TRANSFORMING SOCI

Social work and sociology

Vicky Price and Graeme Simpson

Consultant editor: Jo Campling

First published in Great Britain in 2007 by

The Policy Press
University of Bristol
Fourth Floor
Beacon House
Queen's Road
Bristol BS8 1QU
UK

Tel +44 (0)117 331 4054
Fax +44 (0)117 331 4093
e-mail tpp-info@bristol.ac.uk
www.policypress.org.uk

British Library Cataloguing in Publication Data
A catalogue record for this book is available from the British Library.

Library of Congress Cataloging-in-Publication Data
A catalog record for this book has been requested.

ISBN 978 1 86134 741 1 paperback
ISBN 978 1 86134 742 8 hardcover

Cover design by Qube Design Associates, Bristol.
Front cover: photograph supplied by kind permission of www.third-avenue.co.uk
Printed and bound in Great Britain by MPG Books, Bodmin.

Contents

Acknowledgements

Many people have helped in the writing of this book, some have hindered. Of course, what remains is the authors' responsibility but special thanks go to Stuart Connor, for his ideas on the importance of the dialectic; Dave Denham, for his encouragement, belief in the importance of classical sociology, and for reading some of the early drafts; Ani Murr, who read through all the drafts, when she could have been watching Liverpool or Shrewsbury Town play football or taking her dog for a walk; Judith Holt, who tried her best to give us time away from teaching to write this; Paul Grant, who encouraged us to develop the ideas; Ann Davis in the first instance; and Margot Levinson, who had her own wonderful way of keeping everything in context!

Becky thought of an alternative title, which wasn't used, and Sarah kept asking about how things were going. Ollie, is glad that it's all finished, and he can get the computer back, while Michael provided inspiration for some of the material. Tom spent most of the time in the Middle East and James is always remembered.

Finally, thanks go to the late Jo Campling and staff at The Policy Press for their encouragement, help and advice; our students, of course, who have helped us to develop ways of presenting the material in an accessible manner and who have given us help and ideas far beyond what they could have imagined; but, above all, to *our* teachers and all those involved in the struggle for a better world.

Vicky Price and Graeme Simpson, November 2006

Introduction

The authors have been teaching sociology (and, for that matter, social work) for nearly 30 years, many of which were spent in practice. One of the shifts that has been apparent in social work during this period has been the move towards an office-based bureaucracy. During discussions about the nature of social work with students, and practitioners undertaking post-qualifying programmes, the authors have become acutely aware of how little direct contact many social workers have with service users, and that sociology has only minimal impact on their practice. As a result, the authors have developed an approach to the teaching of sociology and its relevance for social work that is reflected in this book.

The approach has been well received. Many students have commented, however, that although the ideas are accessible and relevant (because they are located in the real world), they are not always easy to grasp (because that is the nature of sociology, trying to explain the commonplace). Above all, the book was written because the authors have a strong desire to rekindle what C. Wright Mills (2000) famously termed 'the sociological imagination' in today's generation of social workers.

As noted above, this book came out of the authors' teaching and it is designed to be as accessible as possible to all readers. Students begin courses full of enthusiasm and this is to be encouraged, but the authors were presented with the problem of how to maintain accessibility when the material within the book was so varied in its complexity. In addition, not all readers respond in the same way. In order to make the material as accessible as possible, the authors have used relaxed and informal language throughout the book. Another technique used is to ask questions, inviting the reader to engage in activities. A third is to provide short 'case studies' or vignettes that draw on people's experiences – either as carers or social workers. Finally, there is more complex academic discussion and explanation when the material demands it. Although this results in a combination of styles, the hope is that the book will be read sympathetically, allowing for the fact that readers will respond differently. One colleague commented that it reads like a discussion, at times easy-going, at others telling stories and recounting experiences, and sometimes becoming very intense. That is how it is in real life.

Introductions clarify general terms of reference and set out what you are going to do, why and how you are going to do it. This is good advice for writing essays and completing assessed tasks, and it underpins the very tasks that those involved in social care work at all levels undertake. With that in mind, this section starts by trying to clarify what certain terms mean – 'trying', because not all terms have exactly the same set of shared meanings.

Social work and social care

What is social work and how is it different to social care? First, these are terms that are very country-specific. Activities that are termed 'social work' in some European countries, for example, are seen differently in the UK. In Germany, there is a national organisation of 'fan projects'. These projects exist at all professional football clubs and are organised and staffed with social workers. At the Borussia Dortmund fan project, for example, there are five full-time members of staff: three qualified social workers, an accountant and a director of sporting activities (www.fanprojekt-dortmund.de). The aim of such projects is, first, to ensure safe and trouble-free matches, and, second, to provide support and advice to fans who are experiencing difficult times in their lives. Such projects do not exist in the UK, and even if they did the staff would be unlikely to have the title 'social worker'.

To make matters of definition more complex, what was once seen as 'social work' in the UK is now often described as 'social care'. Staff who work in residential care in the early 21st century are regarded primarily as 'social care staff', whereas in the 1970s they would have been seen as 'residential social workers'. The title 'social worker' in the UK has only been protected since the establishment of the General Social Care Council (GSCC) and processes of registration, open since 2004. Yet, the GSCC regulates *all* social care staff.

The Department of Health website defines social care as follows:

> Social care comes in many forms, such as care at home, in day centres
> or by way of residential or nursing homes. The term also covers services
> such as providing meals on wheels to the elderly, home help for people
> with disabilities and fostering services. (www.dh.gov.uk/)

The same website, though, soon begins to conflate social care with social services, which, of course, includes social workers.

In the authors' opinion, social care workers provide a set of services, for which social workers have usually undertaken an assessment and subsequently manage the multidisciplinary nature of these services. There are not only cross-national differences, but also more local differences, that can be detected in the titles of various roles; for example, some local authorities have education social workers, while others do not.

These differences, while important in some contexts, are less so in the context of this book, which attempts to introduce sociological concepts to the understanding of how people's lives are affected by the nature of society. It is therefore important to see that, whatever their title, the concepts are important to all those who are employed in working with the poor, the socially excluded and the marginalised in society. For the most part, however, the term social work is used here to refer to a wide range of services, both in terms of assessment and their implementation. This approach follows a broadly European definition, rather than the narrower and contested UK definition.

Sociology and social work practice

Sociology is the study of society. For this reason, it is an essential part of the social worker's academic and *practice* training. Over the years, social work has lost much of its sociological impulse and has come to focus on the personalised aspects of the social work task, indeed to the extent where sociology has almost disappeared from aspects of the curriculum (O'Brien, 2004). It is hoped that this book will go some way to addressing this, since the authors believe that sociology is crucial to understanding both the role of social work in society, and actual social work practice.

Social workers encounter people who are income-poor, socially excluded and live on the margins of society. Without a sound understanding of the type of society that these people live in, social work runs the risk of responding to their situation in a way that individualises their troubles and ignores the nature of social structures. Immediately, this approach causes a potential conflict for the social worker. Are they not supposed to work with people who have *individual* 'needs'? Of course, this is the case, but to ignore what has generated those 'needs' is to miss out on a significant set of factors.

A cursory review of the social work literature reveals a tension between approaches drawn from psychology (for example, Howe, 1987, 1995; Coulshed, 1988, Howe et al, 1999), those drawn from practice (for example, Hardiker and Curnock, 1979; Davies, 1985; Erath and Hämäläinen, 2001) and those influenced by sociology (for example, Bailey and Brake, 1975; Lee, 1982; Day, 1987; Davies, 1991; Jones and Novak, 1993). Dominelli (1997) develops an anti-racist and feminist sociological perspective and offers an analysis of social work as an organised profession. Cree (2000) examines sociology in relation to a range of service user groups, and tellingly notes that:

> Sociological voices have remained on the edge of mainstream social work theory and knowledge, struggling to be heard above the predominantly individual, psychological and correctional discourses in social work. (p 4)

Reamer (1993, p 36) also identifies this potential area of conflict and contradiction within social work. He argues that on one side stand those professionals who believe the main aim of social work is to seek structural change to deal with problems such as poverty, whereas at the other extreme there are those whose approach is located in clinical, personalised services. He concludes that this is a tension between the 'common good' and 'public interest', and is common to many, if not all, of the welfare professions.

There is a range of disciplines that are relevant to social work practice, and this includes sociology as an *integral* part of practice and not an 'add-on' or optional extra. We start from the position that social workers are involved with those people who are marginalised by society, the poor and socially excluded. To work in this arena, an understanding of how these phenomena are generated is essential and sociology offers this perspective. Social workers need to understand how structures create individual problems, otherwise they will effectively "abandon their clients" (Jones, 1997, p 33).

Which sociology?

This is an important question to deal with at the onset. There are many forms of sociological insights, from the classical sociology of Marx, Weber and Durkheim, through to feminism, structuralism, discourse theories and postmodernism. So, any text such as this has to make choices, otherwise it is likely to become little more than a compilation of a range of competing theoretical positions.

The approach here is to explore the nature of contemporary society and its economic underpinnings. Denham (2005) argues persuasively that classical sociology has much to offer in how it can be used to understand current society. The early writers had a clear focus on how the nature of capitalist development was essential to an understanding of how people's lives were affected by the economic demands of capital. This book also adopts an analysis of contemporary society that is located within economic structures.

This reflects a concern with the themes of poverty, social exclusion and inequality, and a strong belief that these are questions that need a central place in the social work agenda. Thus, much of this book is concerned with theories that have been described as 'modernist', although postmodernism is not entirely absent, especially the work of Bauman in relation to consumption.

By exploring the economic nature of society, the book is also able to explore the question of social work as *work*, something that seems to have been overlooked since the radical social work literature of the 1970s (for example, Bailey and Brake 1975; Corrigan and Leonard, 1978) and replaced by a focus on organisational structures (Day, 1987; Davies, 1991; Dominelli, 1997). This book therefore uses sociological theories that can be applied to what social workers do and how they do it and, most importantly, in understanding the life situations of those who are the recipients. In this regard, sociology has a dangerousness for social workers, something that was understood by the radicals of the 1970s. It prises open the contradictions inherent in society and places social work in an uncomfortable place, as 'in and against the state' (for an example of this, see City of Coventry CDP, 1975).

The book is organised in clear sections. In each section, the first chapter will deal with the sociological theory, linking this to society. The subsequent chapter will apply this to social work practice, beginning with a discussion of social exclusion and poverty to establish these as key themes in the text, subsequently demonstrating how social work has always been concerned with the poor and socially excluded. The next stage is to consider four areas of sociological investigation: production, reproduction, consumption and community. In less sociological language, the key areas are:

- work – how we spend a great proportion of our lives and how we earn money, or not, as the case may be;
- relationships – the time spent in homes, families, and how our private lives serve to 'reproduce' the type of people needed to go out and work;
- shopping – how we spend our money and the meaning this holds for us;
- community – where we live and what our social networks are.

Not only are these substantial areas of sociology, they are also areas that are *inclusive*. They have an impact on everyone, irrespective of ethnicity, gender, disability, sexuality or any other difference. In fact, the authors originally viewed these concepts as 'work, sex and shopping'. These concepts can be used to think about people's stories and histories, charting how people's lives have changed over generations with regard to work, sex and shopping. This is also useful for social workers involved with older adults, who have life stories rooted in different times.

While recognising the contribution of the politics of difference and identity, a clear claim can be staked here for the importance of poverty, exclusion, class and economic analyses, and a politics that seeks to unite people, according to what they have in common. Ferguson and Lavalette (2004, pp 298-9), in their defence of Marx, identified some of the criticisms of a Marxist – which could be extended to incorporate a classical sociological – position, expressing a view that in some circles it would be seen as "at best antediluvian and misguided, at worst, a wicked attempt to re-impose, in the jargon, a totalising, euro-centric grand narrative".

Their defence is not reiterated here in full; it is sufficient to stress their observation that much of the social work literature from 1990 onwards has downplayed the structural oppression many service users face. This may not have been the intention, but the use of postmodern concepts has led to a shift away from structural inequality (Noble, 2004). What this book aims to do is: to demonstrate that classical sociological accounts emphasise structural inequalities, oppression and exploitation; to stress the importance of human action; to re-emphasise the importance of the social (or collective), as opposed to the individual; and, finally, to offer the prospect of change.

The focus is not solely on Marxism, but embraces a revised understanding of Durkheim's sociology (Stedman Jones, 2001), and includes other perspectives in an analysis of relationships, consumption and community. This approach is grounded in an analysis of capital – following Marx – and the authors believe that it is time for this to find its way back on to the social work agenda, by bringing to the fore an analysis that shows how recent transformations have sought to mask the economic realities of 21st-century capitalism.

Transforming society: contradictions and change

'Dualism' and 'dialectics' are terms that occur routinely in sociology and can be quite confusing. The dialectic is central to Marx's sociology, but, as Craib (1997, p 59) points out, the work of other classical sociologists is premised on dualisms – tensions and possible contradictions. This book tries to set these out in ways that make them understandable and allow the reader to make the links with the other material.

The dialectic according to Craib (1997, p 40) contains three elements. First, he suggests that it implies inclusiveness and a totality about society and our knowledge of it. Second, he locates it within Hegel's philosophical thought. The simplified version of this is a process of thesis–antithesis – and synthesis. That is, there is an *initial* proposition, a *counter*-proposition and an *outcome*, which is neither the triumph of the thesis nor the antithesis, but it does become the new thesis, which in its turn is subjected to the process of the dialectic. Thus, the dialectic is a continuing process. The third aspect is contradiction, movement and tensions. Marx argued that capitalism was in a state of constant change and contradictions and that everything is fluid. It is out of these contradictions that changes will come, hence the importance of understanding this in relation to contemporary society.

While the dialectic is inevitably associated with Marx, other sociologists identified aspects of something that Craib terms 'dualism'. For example, Durkheim argues that capitalism allows for the best expression of individual freedom within society, yet, at the same time, the individualised nature of this poses the greatest risk to social integration and 'society' (Durkheim, 1984).

The dialectic is one of those concepts that becomes almost too difficult to grasp, shrouded in philosophical mysteries and usually written about in a language that does nothing to make it more understandable. Craib's work is particularly useful in that he makes it understandable. Rees (1998) has also attempted to clarify almost 200 years of dialectical thinking. So, drawing on the work of Craib, Rees and some original texts, the following section identifies some of the important aspects of the dialectic that will relate to the rest of our book.

First, one of the difficulties we face when we are trying to get to grips with society, or for that matter social work, is that often it seems fragmented and unconnected. The reality is that, despite this outward appearance, there is a whole that all too often is obscured. This is apparent throughout the discussion in the book in one form or another. There is a difference between 'appearance' and 'reality' and often what we see on the surface hides a deeper 'reality'.

Second, conflict and contradictions are part of the world we live in. Whatever changes are brought about, these only hide underlying realities. As anyone who has undergone departmental restructuring will know, the outward appearance might change, but the underlying problems often remain. Eventually, this leads to another 'restructuring' or 'realignment' within the same organisation.

Third, as we can see from this example, nothing is static. The nature of capitalist organisation is such that it has to be fluid. This is one of its contradictions, for the lack of stability poses its greatest threat – hence the apparent obscuring of certain 'realities'.

What is described here in a relatively simplified form is how the dialectic is a transforming force in society, because it works within the tensions or dualisms that exist. As noted above, one of the criticisms of classical sociology is the view that it is *deterministic*. What this means is that actions of people are determined by other forces, or that people are passive recipients of change. To use another term, is there *agency*, that is, 'human action'?

Gramsci (2003, pp 378-472) makes an important contribution here. He sees the dialectic in terms of interactions between people and their situations that are constant restatements of the principle of thesis–antithesis and synthesis. One of the traditional Hegelian ideas, utilised by Marx and other theorists, is the so-called shift from 'quantity to quality'. Essentially, what this means is that small pieces of action, which have their own meaning and purpose, can become the driving force behind social transformations. Gramsci's vital contribution is that these are not forces in themselves, but rather are completely dependent on the actions and activities of people. Transformation, on whatever level, therefore, only comes about when people intentionally put themselves in the dialectic process. Thus, the whole nature of transformation is completely dependent on human action, or agency.

Durkheim's dualisms are also removed from the realm of social determinism. While his sociology focused on aspects of the 'collective', it was also premised on the role of individuals within that. So, rather than the collective determining individual action, it is the moral actions of individuals that shape how the collective is. So for Durkheim, change is inherent in society, and it is individual and collective activity that is the means of transformation towards a more just social order (Stedman Jones, 2001).

The following chapters attempt to set out a sociology that seeks to present an inclusive whole, through discussing important sociological concepts and their relevance to understanding society. The concepts are then applied to social work. This is the starting point, for it sets out the dialectical forces at work. The aim is to enable readers to see the contradictions in society, the way in which certain 'realities' are obscured by 'appearance' and how underlying all of this is economic organisation.

This is especially relevant for social workers, whose very employment stands in one of capitalism's contradictions. In the 1970s, social workers coined the phrase 'the iron fist in the velvet glove' (Halmos, 1978) to describe the controlling aspect of social work. Yet to see social work as always controlling is to miss the point, since it is frequently an expression of 'care' or, as Halmos (1965), writing in a different era, termed it, 'love'. More recently, there has been a focus on social work having the potential for liberation (Braye and Preston-Shoot, 1995; Izumi, 2005). Thus, social work is continually negotiating a series of tensions, which are identified in a historical analysis in Chapter Two. Above all else, sociology gives a language for this enduring state of social work. Moreover, social work itself as an activity is part of the nature of modern society. For capitalism to 'work', it has to moderate itself and generate systems to encourage 'fairness' and deal with the inequalities it produces. It therefore has to try to preserve itself, in the face of these conflicts and contradictions. Saville (1957) saw the welfare state as an example of this: it provided an element of security for the working class, but it also had to be wrung out of the capitalist class. Thus it was "the price paid [by capital] for political security" (Saville, 1957, p 5).

So, as Craib points out, dualisms, dialectics and conflicts are at the heart of classical sociology. This is useful for modern social workers, whose job, role and tasks are surrounded by tensions and conflicts. While this might be an uncomfortable place for social workers, it is also a real place, and the book tries to identify the situations where social workers are faced with tensions and contradictions – or 'crises'. It is not the intention to reduce the dialectic to a simplistic notion of tensions. If this is all that is achieved, it becomes little more than a personal resolution of a 'dilemma'. However, as social workers are used to seeing and experiencing a series of tensions (or contradictions) in their jobs, this is a good starting point.

This sociological analysis, while not providing the answers, provides a language and a framework to understand the social work role in all its complexity:

> ... the beginning of wisdom is the discovery that there exist contradictions of permanent tension with which it is necessary to live and that it is above all not necessary to seek to resolve. (Gorz, 1982, cited in Cree, 2000, p 205)

By engaging with these crises and contradictions, there is the prospect of change. The resolution of these tensions needs to be played out, however, both in the daily contact with service users and on a broader canvass. The final section of the book seeks to examine the potential for the future of sociology for social work and the profession itself in the light of current conditions. It offers no easy solutions, nor a glib sociological paradigm. It does, however, seek to encourage social workers to embrace the contradictions and crises in their jobs and work for social change.

Part One
Social exclusion, 'the poor' and social work

ONE

Social exclusion and poverty

Defining social exclusion

Social exclusion as a concept has its origins in France (Murard, 2002). The excluded (*les exclus*) referred to those people who were excluded from the main forms of French society and as a result lived on the margins. In many cases, this was quite literally so, as new housing developments were established at the periphery of towns and cities. The rioting in the suburbs of Paris and other French cities in late December 2005/early January 2006 provides evidence of this, as well as some of its consequences. The terminology became adopted within the European Union, and it soon established itself as a broad term to refer to people who lived on the margins, and who either were, or perceived themselves to be, excluded (European Foundation for the Improvement of Living and Working Conditions, 1995).

For those who live on the margins of society, the continuing process of being excluded becomes a daily reality. Individual experiences underline the nature of the exclusion. There is a case, however, for moving beyond the individual to explore how social exclusion is defined.

Burchardt (2000a) argues that an individual is socially excluded if he or she does not participate to a reasonable degree over time in certain activities of his or her society, where this is for reasons beyond his or her control, and where he or she would like to participate. The definition becomes non-specific and inclusion or exclusion results from an individual preference. For example, if there were no desire to participate, using Burchardt's definition there would be no 'exclusion'. A difficulty arises when this is applied to a given situation. Take, for example, the hypothetical situation of Bill and Tom, who are both rough sleepers and for this reason are excluded from certain activities in society. One of these activities could be voting, since without a qualifying address it is difficult to register as a voter. They are both thereby 'excluded'. This is beyond their control, meeting the first aspect of Burchardt's definition. However, while Bill definitely wants to vote, Tom does not. Thus, Bill is socially excluded, Tom is not. It is not difficult to see that their circumstances are the same, but by adding a defining condition of 'wanting to participate', it differentiates between people who share a common experience.

The aspect of volition or desire is not present in the European Foundation's (1995, p 4) definition of "the process through which individuals or groups are wholly or partially excluded from full participation in the society in which they live". Using this definition, both Bill and Tom would be socially excluded. There is a focus here on the notion of process, which we will now examine through the experience of learning disability.

Social exclusion as a process: the case of learning disability

For some groups of people, social exclusion can best be seen as a continuing process. This case study, from a parent whose child has a severe learning disability, identifies some of the factors that made both parent and child marginalised and excluded.

Case study

At birth, rather than celebrating, the family of a learning disabled baby mourns the loss of their 'normal' baby. Friends and extended family keep away, not knowing what to say, and the parents feel revulsion for their newly born, incapable of shaking off negative images associated with the 'subnormality' hospitals of the feeble-minded and imbeciles. The mother in particular might feel shunned by other new mums and fear ridicule or pity. As other babies start to develop, the disabled one lags behind and is perceived as having 'special needs' by professionals, best catered for in specialist settings such as toddler groups. From the age of three the child is likely to be sent to a special school segregated from the rest of society and a significant distance from the child's family and neighbourhood. Rather than encouraging the learning disabled child to walk with others to the local school, a special bus or taxi turns up to the house tooting its horn. This makes sure everybody knows about the 'different' child who lives in the road and it reinforces the message that such children cannot be educated alongside the mainstream kids.

During the holidays, the child finds himself at home in a neighbourhood in which he has made no friends and is viewed as 'different' (the 'kid who is picked up every day in a taxi') and remains isolated and dependent on the family for entertainment and play.

This experience of being excluded lasts throughout the school years and by the time the child becomes an adult he has made very few friends, has gained few or no qualifications, has not learned to deal with the rejection and taunts of the able-bodied and loses out on the structure of the school day. Instead, the child is thrown onto the support of the family at a time when most young people want to hang out with their friends and are thinking about their future away from home. Support from social services in particular is very institutional, offering respite care in residential settings for 18- to 65-year-olds. Support in the form of further education is patchy and rarely matches the hours of parents who work full time.

The negative images this conjures up are a consequence of the processes of exclusion, and not of the disability. The positives should be accentuated, but the reality is one where negative differences are socially reinforced.

In the past, the process of social exclusion was even more extreme, with learning disabled people spending their entire lives in 'subnormality' hospitals. This was in keeping with the general tendency to 'institutionalise' people deemed a problem for one reason or another. For learning disabled people, this treatment was long term and often permanent and it continued to be commonplace for much longer. When it finally ceased, it tended to be replaced by other segregated measures. Today, legislation is such that disabled people have more rights and as a result of their own campaigning services are becoming less segregated. The social model of disability has started to influence the way we understand the discrimination and oppression that disabled people experience and the services people receive (Ryan with Thomas, 1987; Oliver, 1990).

The account above identifies two important areas of social inclusion in relation to social work. First, policies can be developed with the aim of combating exclusion, but these cannot in themselves overcome many of the deeply held views about learning disabled people that are held in society. It also demonstrates that policy development, in the UK and other countries for that matter, is notoriously 'patchy' (Christopher, 1999) and that policy alone cannot be held as a guide to what is actually happening. Second, it shows that in relation to social exclusion, social work can be part of the problem as well as the solution. This is a contradiction within social welfare provision and the dialectical nature of this is a theme that will constantly emerge throughout the book. Social exclusion then impacts on the personal lives of those it affects and it is something that is a continuing process.

Social exclusion and life chances

The Social Exclusion Unit (SEU, 2004a) offers a wide-ranging definition:

> Social exclusion happens when people or places suffer from a series of problems such as unemployment, discrimination, poor skills, low incomes, poor housing, high crime, ill health and family breakdown. When such problems combine they can create a vicious cycle. Social exclusion can happen as a result of problems that face one person in their life. But it can also start from birth. Being born into poverty or to parents with low skills still has a major influence on future life chances. (http://www.socialexclusionunit.gov.uk/page.asp?id=213)

This indicates that there are a number of different and potentially overlapping factors that can lead to exclusion. A brief review of the list is that many, if not most, of the factors are either 'structural' or can be attributed in some part to structural factors. So, here is a definition that acknowledges the process, but adds to it a range of factors which are located in how society is organised.

Esping-Andersen (2002, p 29) suggests that one area of agreement is that social exclusion "occurs when citizens are trapped in inferior life chances". Such a definition can be seen to include most (if not all) definitions of social exclusion. While this definition is brief, it has the advantage of succinctly encapsulating a key aspect. Social exclusion is a phenomenon that can be perpetuated throughout the life course if nothing is done by society to address the reduced life chances.

From these definitions, it becomes clear that social exclusion extends beyond those who either are, or perceive themselves to be, marginalised. It extends to the very fabric of people's long-term life chances and is inextricably linked with the economic workings of society. Returning to the earlier case study, these definitions suggest that learning disabled people are excluded: furthermore, they suggest that the origins of their exclusion have deeper roots than other people's attitudes and welfare policies.

Living on the margins

One way in which the social work literature in particular has identified people who are socially excluded is to refer to them as 'marginalised' or 'living on the margins'. This way of thinking about socially excluded people is useful in that it conjures up images of people on the edge of society, either because of circumstance or choice, or more importantly because others have occupied the mainstream. In other words, marginalisation is not just a state, but also a process that has a focus on those who are doing the 'marginalising'.

This is hinted at in the way that Walker and Walker (1997, p 8) define social exclusion:

> ... the dynamic process of being shut out, fully or partially, from any of the social, economic, political or cultural systems which determine the social integration of a person in society.... [It could be defined as] the denial of ... civil political and social rights of citizenship.

They acknowledge that social exclusion is a process and locate this within the idea of social integration. Thus, in the case study, a learning disabled child and his family are denied many of the opportunities for integration that other children and their families would take for granted. An important aspect of this definition, however, is that social exclusion becomes linked to social rights of citizenship. More critically, there is an indication that this is less to do with preference or circumstance than with being linked to the social actions of other people through the use of the term 'denial'.

Within social work, social exclusion often refers to groups of people who experience some form of discrimination or oppression that impacts on their life chances and/or prevents them from becoming 'full' citizens. Before going any further, consider this question:

Activity

Which groups of people are likely to be 'socially excluded' and in what way are they 'excluded'?

A list drawn up for this activity might have included any or all of the following: women, people from black and minority ethnic groups, gay and lesbian people, disabled people, migrants, lone parents and older people. This is not an exhaustive list, but all these groups have featured in sociological texts that explore the nature of social exclusion (Barry and Hallett, 1998; Byrne, 2002; Chamberlayne et al, 2002; Hills and Stewart, 2005). A question to consider here is what would determine the extent of someone's 'exclusion'. It could be where they live – for example, a black person living in a predominantly 'white' village in rural England may feel they experience higher levels of exclusion than people of a similar ethnic background who live in a city within a clearly discernible community. On the other hand, the same black person may have a higher level of income and be able to experience life in ways in which poorer black inner-city dwellers cannot.

Aspects of exclusion also impact on people's life chances and are evident in different ways during a lifetime. As will be explored in other sections of the book, this could relate to access to healthcare (Sassi, 2005), pre-school education (Glass, 1999; Stewart, 2005), primary and secondary education (McKnight, 2002), higher education (Callender, 2003), work opportunities (McKnight, 2005 provides a comprehensive review) and housing (Dorling and Rees, 2003); to impact on family life (Power and Wilmott, 2005) and to older age (Evandrou and Falkingham, 2005). It is likely that during the activity you will have identified a range of impacts that exclusion could have. You will have realised that social exclusion is a process, which is manifested throughout a person's life in a variety of ways.

Another important aspect of social work is its identification with locality and community. This is a theme that is dealt with comprehensively in Chapter Nine, but it needs to be identified as a feature of social exclusion. While Walker and Walker (1997) argue that it is a dynamic process, Madanipour and colleagues (1998, p 22) suggest that it is a multidimensional process in which various forms of exclusion are combined:

- participation in decision making and political processes;
- access to employment and material resources; and
- integration into common cultural processes.

They go on to argue that the combination of these factors creates acute forms of exclusion that tend to be concentrated in particular neighbourhoods. This analysis links personal and structural factors and opens the level of study into community and society. It suggests that aspects of social exclusion are likely to be located in specific areas and communities within towns and cities.

Silver (1994) identifies three forms of social exclusion, which can be more readily located within a sociological context. First, exclusion can occur when there is a breakdown of the ties between the individual and society. This is termed a solidarity model of social exclusion and can be readily applied to a situation where, for example, an individual may experience some form of illness that renders them isolated and excluded. Second, there is the specialisation model, which results from 'market failure', discrimination or unenforced social rights. For example, in the UK there is legislation to prevent employers discriminating against disabled people. Thus, disabled people have social rights, enshrined in legislation. If, however, these rights are not enforced, employment opportunities will be diminished and, on a personal level, the individual will have no job. The model then rests on an individualised conception of social inclusion or exclusion. Finally, Silver identifies the monopoly model, which results from class, status and political power. This focuses on those who are 'excluding' and reflects the interests of the included, who maintain their monopoly on power and resources.

In a wide-ranging review of social exclusion, Bradshaw (2003) identifies four areas of contemporary society that can give rise to forms of social exclusion. These are the themes of the book, which will systematically explore the sociology around this. Production focuses on the world of work and employment: Bradshaw argues that exclusion in this area, either through unemployment or low pay, is significant, although he also extends this to include exclusion from socially valued activities.

There is also social exclusion from the activities that reproduce capitalism, which Bradshaw terms 'forms of social interaction'. This can be a lack of emotional support or integration with family, friends or community. He also identifies political disengagement as a factor that generates exclusion, and defines this in broad terms as being the lack of involvement in local or national decision making.

As the nature of capitalism has changed from production to consumption, Bradshaw notes how the process of consumption generates forms of social exclusion, reducing the capacity to purchase goods and services, as constrained by low income relative to need.

Social exclusion and poverty

Room (1995a, p 5) is one of the key theorists subscribing to the view that social exclusion is not only different from poverty but is also more of an all-embracing concept that moves away from income inequality. He argues that poverty is primarily focused on distributional issues: the lack of resources at the disposal of an individual or household. Significantly, it is the distribution of resources that is emphasised here and this locates poverty very clearly within an economic analysis of society. Room, however, expands this to argue that social exclusion focuses primarily on relational issues, which he identifies as inadequate social participation, lack of social integration and lack of power. Whether this is a case of 'chicken or egg' has to be a matter of debate. For example, people who are poor, that is, who lack adequate material and financial resources, are also the people who are more likely not to participate socially, are less socially integrated and have less 'power'. In other words, the *results* of poverty are quite likely to be forms of social exclusion, as described and conceptualised earlier.

There is a risk that by focusing on social exclusion, the poverty and the life experiences of 'the poor' are overlooked. Much here depends on the understanding of 'exclusion' and whether or not it is a synonym for 'poverty'. It has been suggested that, as a concept, social exclusion 'depoliticises' poverty, thereby seeing the 'solution' to poverty in developing schemes to promote social inclusion (Byrne, 2002; Searing, 2006). Given that poverty and income inequality are a feature of the society in which we live, and also features in discussions about 'exclusion', it is important to attempt to provide some definitions.

Poverty in itself is a contested term. In basic terms, there is the distinction between 'absolute' and 'relative' poverty. Absolute poverty refers to the basic necessities for subsistence living. The more widely used definition within welfare economies is one of relative poverty. Here, there is a basic acceptance that people should be provided with sufficient means to have the basic necessities met, but that the measure of poverty needs to be one that compares richer with poorer people. An accepted measure of the relative poverty line is 50% of the median of household equivalent income, across the population of any given country (Bradbury and Jäntti, 2001). Thus, by assessing what a typical household may consume and making adjustments for the members of any household, a relative measure of poverty can be calculated for any given country. Such a measure allows for comparisons between countries and also over time (Vleminckx and Smeeding, 2001). Thus, it is possible to identify one of the main differences between poverty and social exclusion virtually straight away: poverty can be *measured*.

Most governments adopt a measure of relative poverty, which in itself is a tacit acknowledgement that there are considerable differences in wealth within any given society. This acknowledges the existence of 'income inequality' within society, while at the same time accepting that the living conditions experienced by the poor in the early 21st century are likely to be much improved in many ways from conditions 100 years ago. Studies of relative poverty have identified a range of factors, which demonstrate how this is the case. One of the first people to assess the extent of relative poverty was Joseph Rowntree at the turn of the 20th century and he developed a list of goods that he considered essential to meet the basic necessities of life. Such measures draw on what is considered essential at a given time, and whether or not they are possessed is an indicator of 'relative' poverty. This means that whilst living standards can gradually improve – for example, there are high rates of television and car ownership across all socioeconomic groups – poverty is measured according to the expectations in a given society at a given time.

Once it is acknowledged that poverty exists, the next question is likely to be 'Why are people poor?'. It is usually the response to this question that determines a government's policy towards the poor. The responses can be polarised into two broad areas: the cause of poverty either lies with the individual (see Murray, 1990, for example), or with the structural factors (see Lister, 2004). The nature–nurture debate is, of course, a fairly simplistic dichotomy, and arguably a number of factors are at play here. These explanations will be considered later in an examination of social work's response to exclusion and poverty, but what it immediately identifies is that while there may be a broad agreement that poverty exists, there is far less agreement about why this is so and, therefore, what to do about it.

Social exclusion or poverty: a social work debate?

The social exclusion–poverty debate, and how to respond to it, is important for social work, with its emphasis on individuals and families. Social exclusion arguably fits more comfortably within a social work agenda than poverty, since there is a tendency within the social exclusion literature to emphasise the excluded at the expense of those who do the excluding (Byrne, 2002). Poverty is more likely to cause social workers to think about the nature of society, which first generates income inequalities from which other inequalities develop. Thus the authors argue that social exclusion, as experienced by most people, is either a direct consequence of this poverty or, in the case of learning disability, likely to be significantly worsened by it.

Returning to the initial exercises, what becomes apparent is that some groups of excluded people may not be 'poor'. The sociological focus of this book leads to the suggestion that the group of people social workers end up being involved with are socially excluded primarily because of their poverty (Jones, 2001). Thus, a disabled person who is also poor is more likely to be the subject of social work intervention than a disabled person with sufficient financial resources. This book also contends that people who are poor are likely to become subject to the concerns of welfare professionals than those who have a more affluent lifestyle. The association of the poor with social problems all too often leads to increased surveillance (Jones and Novak, 1993; Garrett, 1999, 2002, 2004).

Who are the poor?

Anyone can be poor. There are no group characteristics of poor people, but there are some groups of people who are more likely to be poor than others. There has to be a cautionary note here. 'More likely to' usually refers to somebody's chances of being poor and not to the total number of poor people. This would relate to the numbers per 1,000 of the population, for example, or the overall percentage of people from that group. It is also worth noting that within any group there will always be people who are very well off. An obvious example relates to older people. While it is the case that people over retirement age are more likely to be poor than those who are under 65, there are substantial numbers of older people who are very rich, far wealthier than many people of working age. We have identified four groups of people with whom social workers will be concerned who are likely to be poor. This is not an exhaustive list; in particular, people who experience mental ill health are also likely to experience poverty, but the statistical information is often subsumed under other categories.

Retired people are more likely to be poor than those who work (Elchardus and Cohen, 2004). This is, to a degree, unsurprising, since pensions are, generally speaking, a 'fixed income'. The levels of income in retirement are also likely to reflect those during a working life. Thus, the level of income attained while working is a safe indicator of a person's relative wealth during retirement.

Another group of people disproportionately represented among the poor are lone parents (Gregg et al, 1999). In 2001, lone parents headed 22% of all UK families with dependent children; this was three times the proportion in 1971. Although a slight majority (55%) of lone parents are in employment (Palmer et al, 2005), lone-parent families represent the largest number of families who live in poverty through worklessness.

A third group who find themselves more likely than not to be poor are people from black and minority ethnic (BME) groups, especially those from Pakistan and Bangladesh. In their same report, Palmer and colleagues note that 40% of people from BME groups live in poverty, twice the rate than for white people, and one third of all Pakistanis and Bangladeshis earn less than £6.50 an hour (in 2005, the minimum wage was £5.05; in October 2006, it rose to £5.35).

The fourth group is children. Of course, many children will already be included in statistics relating to lone parents and BME groups. They are given separate consideration here, since much social work and welfare provision is explicitly directed at children. In the UK, eradicating child poverty by 2020 is a specific political objective of the New Labour government, with a raft of policy initiatives to reach this goal, built around social capital. There is also welcome focus on children in their own right in their experience of poverty in the work of Ridge (2002).

Understanding exclusion and poverty: the role of sociology

Byrne (2002) locates social exclusion within a society that exploits certain groups of people. His analysis is that certain groups (invariably those who remain poor) are underdeveloped:

> Underdevelopment [is] a good term to use for the actual processes that constitute social exclusion. The socially excluded are those parts of the population who have actively been underdeveloped. (2002, p 55)

By this, Byrne suggests that underdevelopment refers to the systematic reduction and limitation of life chances; therefore, the process of exploitation is central. The clear inference here is that social exclusion occurs, not because individuals and families fail to avail themselves of opportunities, but because opportunities are denied them.

How then should these phenomena be understood? One way of examining this is through the concept of discourse theory (Fairclough, 1992, 1995). Foucault (1977, 1984) locates this within an analysis of power, and, crucially for him, discourses have a 'power' of their own and are not located elsewhere, for example, within the nature of capitalism. Fairclough's analysis, however, suggests that analysing discourse provides a starting point for a wider exploration of the economic and social forces that generate it. Discourse focuses on the mechanisms used to maintain people in a position of subjugation, by the way in which social problems are commonly discussed. In the European Union, there has been a concern over 'asylum seekers' and 'economic migrants' since the beginning of the 21st century. Very often the official language is negative. Thus, the discourse of migration and immigration shapes the way other people perceive the 'other' (Brah, 2001). The questions about discourse will be examined more closely in Chapter Five. At this stage it is sufficient to pose the question: "Does discourse create the ways in which the 'other' is understood, or does it reflect a set of different relationships and mechanisms rooted in the organisation of society?" (Fairclough, 1995).

The approach here is that poverty, or, to use the seemingly preferred term, 'income inequality', needs to be understood with reference to the economic foundation of society. This is not to deny or ignore the place that discourse holds, but rather to ask a different question related to the economic nature of society.

Many of the schemes and initiatives to combat social inequality are couched in terms of 'social inclusion' or 'developing opportunities'. To a large degree, this book concurs with Byrne's (2002) argument that these are neutral terms, seeing 'exclusion' as a depoliticised activity. Indeed, even the use of the term 'income inequality' tends to deflect away from the images associated with 'poverty'. What is needed, however, is not a debate about terminology and engagement with the politics of discourse, but rather an exploration of the nature of society, which generates such inequality. As this book engages with sociological explanations of society, focusing on work (production), relationships (reproduction), what we buy (consumption), how we live (community) and our social networks (social capital), it will argue that these areas form the economic underpinning of contemporary society and are of crucial importance for social workers.

These are dealt with in the following sections, but before engaging in a sociological analysis of society, the relationship between social work and those who live on the margins of society will be established.

TWO

Social work's enduring tensions

This chapter examines how social work has always engaged with people who are poor and socially excluded. Social work, as we currently understand it, has developed over the past 200 years as a response to the difficulties faced by certain groups of people at the onset of industrialisation and capitalism. For much of social work's history, the term 'the poor' has been frequently used to describe these groups. The concept of social exclusion is a late 20th-century development. Nevertheless, social work has a long history of involvement with the poor and dispossessed.

The introduction discussed the concept of the dialectic and argued that the nature of society is one of contradiction, conflict and change. The outcome of the conflict is not simply the triumph of one set of ideas – or one group of people – over another, but something new and distinct. The introduction also emphasised the importance of action and engagement as a force to bring about change. The social workers here operated in the Victorian period, at the onset of industrialisation and large-scale production, characterised by the creation of the modern city and large-scale factory work (Pearson, 1975).

Social work operates on the margins of society and works with those people whose experiences set them apart from the majority, so, in this sense, social exclusion is a useful term to adopt. It has been argued convincingly that social work has always concerned itself with 'the poor' or 'marginalised' (Jones, 2001). This can be traced back to the beginnings of social work in the UK in the late 18th and 19th centuries. Of course, there is a debate to be had as to whether this was merely a mechanism for the control and regulation of the poor (see, for example, Clarke, 1993) or whether it had a more humanitarian aspect (Forsyth and Jordan, 2002). These debates are important for contemporary social workers, and will be explored further. What is in no doubt is that social work deals with people who experience exclusion.

The German writer Engelke (1996, p 7) argued that social work throughout its history had been concerned with "people with whom nobody wants to be bothered"; in other words, social work is specifically concerned with people the rest of society rejects, ignores or is embarrassed by:

> The real role and task of social work is not just to form a link (even though one may not exist) with those who are poor, ill, not cared for, abused, the downtrodden, the victims of persecution, the marginalised,

but to reach out to them, to be bothered about them, to take their
side and to support them. (Engelke, 1996, p 8, authors' translation)

Although some contemporary UK writing puts the issue differently, this is a fair
reflection of the 'reality' of social work and the people with whom it works.
Engelke encapsulates a tension within the social work role and the duality of
modern society. The same society that persecutes people also generates an impulse
to 'do something about it'. This is essentially a human response to a set of human
difficulties. Arguably, Engelke goes further, for he suggests something greater
than a simple human response to those who are 'socially excluded' is needed;
social work has to 'take their side' and this could result in setting the social
worker at odds with others in society.

This has been a constant feature of social work throughout its history. The
form that such action has taken, however, has been contested. The motivation to
engage in social work is located within a moral impulse and Forsyth and Jordan
(2002) locate its origins within the philanthropic tradition. They draw on the
lives of important Victorian women and show how they placed the concern for
the human subject of their interventions above all else. Thus, the moral principles
of valuing other people and treating them with dignity and respect became
established as overriding social work principles, which were reiterated in the
early 1960s (Biestek, 1961). Forsyth and Jordan identified a religious impulse,
but one that essentially valued others and did not seek to moralise, as the driving
force behind the desire to devote one's time to others. Many of the Victorian
women who engaged in social work also sought to change aspects of their
society to improve the life experiences of the groups they worked with.

The initial historical analysis reveals that the instinct to help was not just confined
to the action of helping. It extended to seeking to change aspects of society. The
work of Mary Carpenter (1968) illustrates this. She worked with children and
was especially concerned with those who were on the fringes of criminal activity.
In her book *Reformatory Schools: For the Children of the Perishing and Dangerous
Classes and for Juvenile Offenders*, first published in 1851, she advocated significant
changes to the existing criminal justice and educational system. Among them
were a number of measures built on the principle of universal education and
treating children with respect.

Her main aim was to institute a system of universal education for all children,
arguing that education was the basic foundation of a decent society. She argued
that children who had either committed a crime or were 'at risk' of becoming
involved in crime should be dealt with by way of specialist provision. She
advocated the abolition of corporal punishment for children, on two grounds.
First, it was degrading of both children and the adults who administered it; and,
second, it did not prevent children reoffending. Her final argument was that
children should neither be tried in adult courts nor be imprisoned with adults.

There is little doubt that Carpenter's ideas did not meet overwhelming approval.

This is not to say she did not have some success, since her proposals for 'approved schools' were adopted within six years, and she founded the first, located at Kingswood in Bristol. Muncie (1999) criticises Carpenter for the establishment of the approved school as a restriction on liberty. She certainly benefited from the initial reform in that she was the original pioneer, but Muncie overlooks her other campaigns, which were clearly progressive. Before engaging too heavily in retrospective criticism, it is worth asking whether or not an advocate for such significant reform should be held responsible for the selective and partial implementation of their ideas.

Scull (1984), in his analysis of mental health, develops the notion of 'unintended consequences' of legislation and policy, and this can certainly be applied to Mary Carpenter. Muncie (1999), in his review of youth justice, also draws on the bifurcatory nature of policy in relation to juvenile offenders. This is where the intention of the reform is that the existing measures are replaced, while the reality of political policy implementation is that they essentially add to existing measures, thereby widening the scope of interventions, rather than changing them. Carpenter was arguably one of the first reformers to become a 'victim' of this tendency.

Others commentators see Carpenter in a more favourable light (Watts, 2000) and Forsyth and Jordan (2002) note how her methods were certainly progressive, especially in dealing with behaviour. She was also able to *change* her methods when faced with difficult behaviours without compromising her overall position (Watts, 2000; Forsyth and Jordan, 2002). Significantly, Mary Carpenter had to struggle for her reforms, often against strong opposition from other, usually male, reformers (Watts, 2000, p 47), but she persisted in her belief that all children needed "respect, love and care" to achieve their true potential (Watts, 2000, p 43). In an age where punishment was the dominant response to children and young people's offending behaviour, she brought to the attention of society an alternative approach. Thus, by examining the work of Mary Carpenter with juvenile offenders, we can identify an enduring source of conflict within this area of social work: punishment or treatment?

Carpenter was concerned with engaging in a process of reform, to ensure that her ideas became part of society's response to a set of social problems. The 'intervention' as such was on two levels: first, with the actual children and, second, by engaging with policy. Furthermore, she based her interventions on research of current methods and in that regard they could be termed 'scientific' as well as 'moral'. Carpenter advocated forms of philanthropic intervention, when these were most definitely the subject of considerable criticism. Samuel Smiles (1997, p 1) in his book *Self Help*, first published in 1851, argued that any society (the nation) was an "aggregate of individual conditions, and civilisation itself is but a question of personal improvement". He continued:

> If this view be correct then it follows that the highest patriotism and
> philanthropy consist, not so much in altering laws and modifying
> institutions, but in helping men to elevate and improve themselves by
> their own free and independent action. (Smiles, 1997, p 2)

This is the classical rejection of all forms of intervention and a view that locates
people's difficulties within their personal circumstances. This position is not
confined to the mid-Victorian period; indeed, Margaret Thatcher, the UK's
Conservative Prime Minister (1979-90) who adopted neoliberal policies, held
Smiles to be one of her 'heroes'. Thus, Smiles argues passionately for a non-
interventionist status quo and this reflected a general hostility to those who
engaged in social work at that time. This is the background against which people
like Mary Carpenter struggled. Moreover, the comments are not confined to the
Victorian era and could quite easily be made in a contemporary society, which
often has a negative view of social work and sometimes regards social workers as
'do-gooders'.

The campaign for universal education, however, was widely supported, although
there is evidence that it was not always welcomed by the working classes, who
saw children as a valuable source of income without which the family would
struggle financially. Progressive Factory Acts and legislation that limited the work
children could do left more and more young people at risk of engaging in
criminal activity and it is interesting to note that many commentators argue that
it was this, alongside the need for a more highly skilled workforce, rather than
any moral argument for education, that eventually led to the Education Acts of
1870 and 1880, which set the basis for universal education. However, working-
class resistance remained, largely on economic grounds, since the working poor
needed the income from their children's labour (Cohen, 1981).

While such campaigns had a broad base of support, the general plight of the
poor, whether 'working' or not, was even more contested within this period, and
yet large numbers of philanthropic women (and men) were engaged with these
groups in what can only be seen as social work. The nature and causes of poverty
were contested. Smiles' view dominated: the poor were poor because of their
own lack of moral character, and interventions that supported them would only
serve to generate dependency. There was a widespread fear that this would
somehow result in a catastrophe for society as a whole, as Arnold White wrote in
1887:

> Charity and sanitary regulations are keeping alive, in our large towns,
> thousands of persons who would have died fifty years ago ... Public
> or private charity may alleviate their misery, but the only remedy is
> to prevent such persons coming into existence ... persons of any
> rank who are not in good physical and mental health have no moral
> right to have children. (White, cited in Stedman-Jones, 1984, p 287)

By the latter part of the century, even Smiles had revised his position somewhat, arguing for intervention and education to preserve the position of the middle classes in the face of a growing working class (Stedman-Jones, 1981).

It is in these writings that we can identify aspects of the Victorian fear of class conflict and revolution, which gave an added impetus to much philanthropic activity, though with a more overt agenda related to either social control or placation. This gives rise to one of social work's enduring internal conflicts: that of 'care or control'. The work of Octavia Hill in the provision of social housing illustrates this dichotomy quite clearly. Hill was deeply concerned that a feature of the poor was the absence of decent housing, which led to all manner of 'immoral behaviour' (Whelan, 1998, p 5).

Hill used her wealth to purchase houses, provide substantial improvements to them and then rent them out at affordable, low rents to working people. Her actions in providing such housing were clearly progressive, yet she was subject to criticism because of her methods. The tenants were expected to ensure that the houses were well maintained and with high levels of cleanliness. So, the progressive policy – an aspect of care – was conditional on certain behaviours – an aspect of control. The emphasis seemed to be more on the control than the care. This said, she was also willing to offer whatever help she could and insisted that the poor were treated with the utmost respect, an early example of Biestek's social work value of respect to all persons (1961):

> I should give them any help I could, such as I might offer without insult to other friends.... I am convinced that one of the evils of much that is done for the poor springs from the want of delicacy felt, and courtesy shown towards them, and that we cannot beneficially help them in any spirit different to that in which we help those who are better off. (Hill, cited in Whelan, 1998, p 7)

Hill was associated with another group of Victorian social workers who formed themselves into the Charitable Organisation Society (COS). Much has been written about this movement, and much of it is negative. An enduring legacy for social work, however, has been an emphasis on assessment and record keeping. It is also noteworthy that the COS assessed according to stated criteria. These focused mainly on three aspects: first, it had to be the only source of help available; second, the proposed recipient had to be 'deserving' of the intervention; and, third, the intervention had to benefit the recipient (Whelan, 2001). Some of the interventions were innovative, to say the least:

> After getting a man to sign the pledge, the committee thought it only right to supply him at home with a gramophone, to counteract the siren strains of a neighbouring public house. (Muirhead, 1911, p 259)

The work of the COS brought into focus the debates of the late 19th century and the response to the poor and poverty. On the one hand, there were those who saw poverty as being mainly the result of a lack of morality, or 'fecklessness'. Against these were those who saw the problem as being rooted in the social system. This group acknowledged that poverty – and not immorality – was the cause of, among other things, heavy drinking. A Scottish churchman argued that:

> If intemperance is often the cause ... [of poverty] ... I assert it as often the consequence of these conditions of living. (MacLeod, 1888, reproduced in Moore, 1988, p 285)

Lidgett, another churchman involved in late 19th-century social work, stated that he was "not willing that [the Church] should be merely an ambulance to gather up the casualties of our industrial system, without being equally anxious to lessen the causes of those casualties" (Lidgett, cited in Heaseman, 1962, p 62). A socialist colleague was even clearer about what the role of organised religion should be:

> The day is past when we could treat a man as a brother when concerned with the salvation of his soul, and be content to leave him as a bond-slave or machine when social and economic interests are concerned. (Henderson, cited in Heaseman, 1962, p 66)

While these statements come from figures associated with the Church, it is important to remember that much – if not almost all – Victorian social work was organised around religious organisations. This was, after all, a society where regular church attendance was around 70%. The concerns expressed, however, neatly encapsulate another enduring tension within social work: individual faults or structural factors?

The lack of an organised state response saw the creation of specific societies for the alleviation of poverty among minority groups. Two groups within Victorian society were particularly noticeable as disadvantaged minorities: the Jewish and Irish (Roman Catholic) communities. Each group developed its own responses, partly to alleviate poverty and partly to sustain a particular sense of identity. A fine example of this was the Saint Vincent de Paul Society in Glasgow, which through a combination of cultural and charitable activities "created and sustained the tight-knit 'cradle to grave' community of the late Victorian urban Catholic ghetto ... [to the extent that] ... it was described as a welfare state within the state" (Parsons, 1991, p 174).

While the organisation of social work to alleviate the plight of the poor was a central feature of Victorian society, it was not the only factor and other political movements emerged. The Chartist movement had some success in establishing limited voting rights for working men, and by the latter part of the century the trades union movement in the UK had become stronger, with links to European socialist and communist parties. In part, it was this that led to the fears expressed by Smiles and others as they saw their privileged position in society threatened. Stedman-Jones (1984), in his seminal work *Outcast London*, identifies the rise of the working-class movement, culminating in the strikes of 1888: first, the matchgirls, led by Annie Besant, followed by the dockers. Stedman-Jones points to the broad base of support for these strikes and concludes that by 1890 the trades union movement had effectively moralised itself, so that organised labour posed no threat to the security of the state, as Smiles had feared. However, figures such as Henderson and Lidgett were significant in engaging with the Labour movement to bring about wider changes to society. Thus, we can identify another enduring dilemma for social work and social workers: the extent of engagement with the political process and developing a collective strategy.

So far this chapter has set out some of social work's historical and enduring tensions:

• Punishment or treatment?
• Care or control?
• Individual faults or structural factors?
• The extent of engagement with the political process and developing a collective strategy.

These questions arise from the particular position of social work and are evident in contemporary social work practice. So, who are 'the excluded' and 'the poor' that the social workers engaged with in Victorian times and continue to be the focus of intervention more than 100 years later? The 19th century saw an extensive range of interventions with a wide-ranging set of people. Heaseman (1962) undertakes a comprehensive review of social work in Victorian times and identifies the full extent of the provision. In looking at her categorisations, the striking feature is the enduring nature of the 'target groups'. The similarity of the two groups adds more weight to the argument that 'social exclusion' has its origins in the organisation of society and more explicitly in a feature of industrial capitalism.

Victorian social work	Contemporary social work
Elderly people	Older people or elders
The deserving poor	Provision for income maintenance is through welfare state provision.
The ill and dying	The ill and dying: hospital social work and the hospice movement
Prostitutes (fallen women)	Social work with 'sex workers' through outreach to 'streetworkers'
Children, especially the abused	Children – abused children still form a significant share of childcare social work.
Mentally ill and disabled people	Mental health social work; social work with disabled people. In the UK, these form two separate service user groups.
Unemployed people	While unemployment is not a feature of social work, unemployed people have a personal adviser to encourage them into employment.
Soldiers and sailors	The Soldiers, Sailors, Airmen and Families Association (an independent organisation) provides services to former service personnel.
Children in need of education	The education social worker is almost exclusively engaged with children who do not attend school.
Juvenile delinquents	Youth Justice teams continue to work with young offenders, though there is less of a focus on prevention.
'Alcoholics'	There is a significant amount of social work directed towards people who misuse substances, including alcohol.
Prisoners	The probation service continues to work with this group of people, both in prisons and on release.

We can see that social workers have been concerned with the same type of difficulties faced by people in the UK for more than 150 years. Social workers have always been involved with children, whether their involvement is related to abuse, criminality, education or, more recently, the notion of 'need'. Likewise, there has always been some degree of involvement with disabled people, those who experience mental ill health and those who experience chronic illnesses and are near the end of their lives (a recent development in this area of work is the hospice movement). Other areas appear to be heavily located in a particular morality, most notably work with 'prostitutes' and 'alcoholics', while others have been taken over by more obvious welfare state provision, for example, the provision of relief to the poor and the unemployed. Nevertheless, the consistency of the 'service user group' is remarkable. The people targeted by social work intervention have always been those we would now term 'socially excluded'. The enduring nature of social problems takes us straight to the heart of one of the tensions within social work, identified earlier as individual faults or structural factors.

If these groups of people have been the recipients of social work or social welfare services from the onset of industrial capitalism in the UK, is this because the problems are an essential part of the human condition and located in a range of individual factors or is it that the problems have causations that are more likely to be located within social structures? This is not intended as a simplistic nature–nurture dichotomy. It is now accepted that there is, at the very least, an interplay of factors at work. This does not resolve the problem for social workers, for it becomes a question of *how* social workers *choose* to define the difficulties their service users face. There is a tendency to view early social work as being highly moralistic and focused almost exclusively on the individual, and to contrast this with a more enlightened late 20th-century approach (for example, Clarke, 1993; Corby, 1993; Dominelli, 1997). It was not always the case that those who brought about improvements sought collective solutions. Mary Carpenter, though fully aware of the structural factors that brought about poverty, and the differential ways children of lower classes were treated, campaigned around her view that education would be the best response to poverty (Watts, 2000). A review of the strong link between education and social capital (undertaken in Chapter Ten) shows the extent to which such a view has persisted. Tensions have always been present in social work and welfare work, and the more important question is: where do social workers choose to place their emphasis?

Part Two
Production

THREE

Theories of work and society

This chapter will introduce the concept of production, by exploring the sociological contributions of Marx and Durkheim to the study of work in a capitalist society. The impact of changing patterns of paid work (including patterns of male and female employment) will be analysed in this framework. Finally, alienation will be introduced and discussed as a concept of importance in the study of work and society.

What is production?

The concept of production has a lengthy history within sociology and one of the first writers who dealt with the subject was Karl Marx. Marx argued that production is essential to human survival and that we all need to produce; the term has come to be related to both the process and organisation of production. A more accessible way to understand the concept is to think about work.

> **Activity**
>
> Think about your own work and write down the different ways it could be described. Do not dwell on the specific tasks you undertake, but think more widely about it.

Work can be conceptualised in a number of ways:

- As an activity – this is quite simply what we do. Social workers, for example, may undertake many different activities as part of their job, such as visiting people, attending meetings, filling in forms, writing reports and going to court.
- As a process – this includes all of the above as part of a continuing process in, for example, ensuring the safety of a child. The process also includes contact with other people within the place of work, including supervisors.
- As organisation – this focuses on how the work is organised and includes management structures and aspects of managerial and organisational control.

You will probably recognise that social workers do not actually 'produce' anything that other people would recognise as a 'product', unlike someone who works in a car factory. Such a person, who might have a specific task, is part of a process in the overall production organised and controlled to produce the end product – a car. This takes us to an aspect of modern society that creates a new set of debates about work and production. There are many jobs in the developed world that were not even envisaged in the society Marx analysed. Nonetheless, Marx's writings are an important place to begin to understand the relationship between people and their work. During the discussion that follows and for the rest of the book, the term capitalism is used. This is for two main reasons: first, it was the term used by Marx to identify the type of economic organisation in the 19th century, and, second, it has been an enduring feature of the economic order since. Of course, Western societies have changed, yet the fundamental feature of economic organisation throughout the world, especially since the collapse of the Soviet Union, is capitalism. Carruthers and Babb (2000) suggest that not all capitalist societies have the same level of market organisation. In addition, Esping-Andersen (1990) argued that within industrial capitalist countries there were different types of welfare regimes, yet whatever the outward differences, the dominant economic organising force remains one of capitalism. It is to Marx's analysis of this that we now turn.

Conflict or consensus?

Surplus value and class exploitation

Marx believed that the nature of humanity was collective, and that capitalism had not only intensified competition between people in the pursuit of profit and freedom, but also resulted in massive inequalities between rich and poor. To make matters worse, any sense of social obligation had been removed and old social bonds had been 'ripped asunder' (Marx and Engels, 1992). One of Marx's key philosophical and analytical concepts was explored in the introduction (the dialectic) and this is important for understanding the essence of conflict that Marx identifies within all societies. It could be suggested that at the heart of Marx's analysis is the concern for human freedom and equality, arguing that "people cannot be liberated as long as they are unable to obtain food and drink, housing and clothing in adequate quality and quantity" (Marx, 1964, p 56 in Jordan, 1972, p 279). Central to this, however, is his analysis of capitalist society.

Marx's analysis of capitalism rests on the idea that people's work activity (labour) has been turned into a commodity and given a monetary value. The products they make have a different monetary value. The work undertaken, therefore, becomes a commodity that can be bought (by the employer) and sold (by the worker) but that crucially is subject to market forces. The products sold in a capitalist society are commodities and they are created through the employer investing in their production with raw materials and the machinery needed to make the goods and through employing human labour power (people). The goods are produced for profit, which goes to the employer, and they are not produced for the direct use of either the employer or employees. In this way, the work activity and its process result in a product the workers may neither want, need, nor be able to afford. In *Capital* (Marx, 1990), which was first published in 1867, Marx engages in a lengthy and complex account of the relationship between labour, capital and commodities. He argues that a commodity has both a use and an exchange value. The use value is attained in the product's consumption and this helps determine its exchange value. Marx then developed the concept further to give a relative value to this, which in the final analysis includes labour value, the work needed to produce an article "under the conditions of production normal for a *given society* and with the average degree of skill … prevalent *in that society*" (Marx, 1990, p 129, emphasis added). Marx was not saying that the nature of capitalism would remain static; rather, the expression of the relationship would be rooted in a particular phase of capitalist development, and its value determined according to those conditions.

Marx then was able to identify the nature of 'surplus value'. The worker, in a capitalist economy, is able to sell their labour power – the ability to create a commodity with a use value – for a wage. The product created will then have a value greater than the outlay in wages. Notionally, Marx saw the working day as being divided into two; the first part was the labour needed to create the product; the second the labour needed to create the capitalist's profit. This is the creation of surplus value (Marx, 1990). In short, the employer exploits the labour power of their employees in the pursuit of profit. The nature of the economic and work relationship is one of exploitation.

For Marx, however, this was not simply an individual contract that was entered into. Society came to be shaped by the nature of the economic relationship and organised to this end. The most straightforward account of this can be found in the Communist Manifesto, originally published in 1848 (although not published in England for almost another 50 years). This is essentially a polemical work, which was hastily written to spur on a series of revolutions in Europe in that year. To that end, it is but a simplified version of Marx's theories about the development of human societies, and established his view that in every economic period there are two classes that stand in opposition. Under capitalism, these are the 'bourgeoisie' and the 'proletariat'. The bourgeoisie are those who own the 'means of production and exchange' and the proletariat are those who can only live by selling their labour, a class of wage labourers.

There are two important points to make about classes within the Marxist analysis. First, there are more than two classes. Marx fully understood that there were a number of class groups, and that this had always been the case. What he and subsequent writers argue is that these different class groups have to decide where they will put their allegiance (Poulantzas, 1978; Marx, 2005). Second, these should not be confused with the more contemporary concepts of 'middle' or 'working' class. The crucial factor is the nature of the relationship to production or work.

There is also a lengthy literature about the nature of classes and class development under capitalism (Poulantzas, 1978; Gramsci, 2003). Marx argued that the end result would be the overthrow of capitalism and its replacement by an economic system that rejects the market, where forms of production are created in conditions of freedom from exploitation and regulated by the people who are themselves engaged in the production. The nature of class analysis, socialism and revolution are themselves the subject of a lengthy literature within Marxism. It is not the intention to explore elements of this debate here, but rather to identify the key points that emerge from Marx's analysis of capitalism:

- It is a system based on profit where labour is reduced to just another commodity that has a monetary value.
- The nature of the work relationship is an exploitative one.
- It is the relationship between production and labour that creates the type of society we live in and that society is organised for the benefit of the capitalist.

Cohesion and fulfilment?

Social solidarity and the division of labour

Like Marx, Durkheim[1] began from the position that the essential nature of people was to live and work collaboratively: as people, we are social beings and our desire is to live in a sense of harmony with others. Durkheim argued that society is held together by a set of social ties or bonds, and he observed that the development of modern capitalist society had fundamentally changed this (Durkheim, 1984; Stedman Jones, 2001). The term 'mechanical solidarity' referred to a relatively small-scale organised society where all people were bonded together by self-evident common interest, often cemented by religious belief and cultural norms, with little inequality. While such societies may still be found in more remote parts of the world, it is not the intention to dwell here on this aspect of Durkheim's work. Of more interest is what Durkheim wrote about capitalist society and how the 'social' is created and maintained under different economic conditions. He termed this 'organic solidarity'. Here the bonds between people are looser and the collective sense under greater threat from a number of factors.

First, the division of labour leads to a different level of dependency. People are reliant on others to perform tasks they cannot do themselves. This division of labour in itself can lead to a sense of interdependence and social bonds. So, whereas in mechanical solidarity the key factors in maintaining society were kinship and religious ties, resulting in shared values, under capitalism it is the fact that we are all mutually dependent on one another that generates cohesion. Capitalism and the division of labour also bring about much greater levels of human freedom, based on status and occupation rather than on religious or family ties (Durkheim, 1983). So Durkheim's sociological account of capitalism is generally positive, since it offers the opportunities for greater freedom and fulfilment. This is in contrast to Marx, who saw the division of labour as being the fundamental aspect of capitalism that generated great potential for exploitation.

Durkheim, therefore, sees the potential within capitalism for individuals and this generally positive view has often resulted in criticisms of his sociology. Stedman Jones (2001) suggests that this needs further exploration and notes that Durkheim went on to suggest that without suitable controls, capitalism would destroy social solidarity. Through its competition and desire for profit it led to a focus on the individual at the expense of society. Durkheim was of the view that this would lead to a distancing of people from society and destroy the very solidarity that capitalist society needed. Here, then, lies the dualism: while the individual is important and seeks fulfilment, this is done within the framework of 'society', that is, a sense of collective living (Giddens, 1978; Craib, 1997). Durkheim called the collective organisation of capitalism *'socialisme'*. It needs to be stressed that while this translates as 'socialism', it is of a different nature to that proposed by Marx. Durkheim opposed revolutionary transformation for many reasons, but a key one was that, in France, successive revolutions had been followed by counter-revolutions that had led to even more reactionary governments (Stedman Jones, 2001). He was interested in how a fairer society could be brought about within France, while maintaining solidarity, through what we now regard as social democratic means. Nevertheless, he argued that only in an equal society could genuine organic solidarity be brought about. Thus, Durkheim's sociological understanding of capitalism saw a dualism and contradiction that could only be addressed through promoting equality. While Marx saw capitalism as the antithesis of human freedom because of the levels of inequality it created, Durkheim saw within it the potential for greater human freedom. His writing was concerned with exploring how individuals could attain greater levels of freedom and yet maintain something we would call 'society'. Durkheim was concerned about the development of capitalism and predicted that through the continuation of the division of labour there would be 'ever-growing inequality' (Stedman Jones, 2001, p 104). The ideal of social justice, therefore, needed to turn into action before true equality and fulfilment could be brought about. Without this, people will experience 'anomie', a "lack of solidarity and social relatedness" (Stedman Jones, 2001, p 102) and the more pronounced the distances between people, as a result of capitalism, the greater their sense of anomie.

Like Marx, Durkheim is a complex writer, whose work has been subject to much debate. It is perhaps fair to say that in more recent times his work has not received the same amount of attention as Marx's, and that he is generally viewed as a sociologist who promotes order and solidarity as opposed to revolution. For this reason, he has become associated with functionalism (see later). However, the main points to emphasise here are:

- People desire social cohesion.
- Capitalism and the division of labour offer greater opportunities for personal fulfilment.
- Without controls, capitalism will promote individualism, and this will destroy social solidarity.
- When people are isolated, the result is 'anomie', but this has its roots in the economic system.

Have things changed?

A criticism of both Marx and Durkheim (and, for that matter, Weber, the other so-called founding father of sociology) is that they wrote about a society that has long since disappeared. It is clear that on the surface society has changed considerably in the past 150 years or so, but is this appearance a sign that the 'nature' of society has also changed to the same extent? The distinction between how things are and how they look is a feature of the dialectic process and it is therefore necessary to explore contemporary views of work and society to examine the extent to which things have really changed.

Functionalism

A sociology frequently associated with Durkheim's analysis, and one that has had significant influence, is that of functionalism. Functionalism is largely a product of the postwar era, specifically the 1950s, when the West was experiencing an almost unprecedented economic boom (Esping-Andersen, 2002). It should be noted that this is only a partial understanding of Durkheim, who himself was associated with French social democracy, and therefore not a 'conservative' as he is often thought to be (for a full discussion of Durkheim and social democratic politics in France, see Stedman Jones, 2001).

Functionalism stems from the premise that within any given society there are a range of phenomena and structures that work together to generate stability. Whatever happens in one area will have an impact on another area, and it is not necessarily the case that people involved in these areas will be aware that they are generating stability. One of the key writers within this school was Talcott Parsons (Parsons, 1951; Parsons and Bales, 1955). The organisation of society, notably the nuclear family, developed to meet the needs of capital. A feature of functionalism is that stratification and inequality is not just inevitable, but necessary. This relates directly to aspects of production, work and inequality, since functionalists would content themselves that some roles in society are more necessary than others and the skills needed for such roles relatively scarce. Thus, greater rewards are needed to encourage the people who possess these skills to utilise them for the benefit of society. The great debate this generates is simply this: who decides what is more necessary and hence more worthy of higher reward? There is a danger that the theory merely becomes a circular argument for the existence of inequality. For example, doctors are highly skilled and trained, and most people would agree that they have a functional necessity to society. However, in relation to the spreading of disease, it could be argued that without the refuse collector, a role that requires less skill and training, disease would be rampant and the doctors' role made impossible. So, it could be argued that the reward levels are not based on social necessity, since in this regard one could not operate without the other.

Functionalism, then, is uncritical of the capitalist nature of society – indeed, its critics formed a sociological school of their own, namely 'conflict theory' (Dahrendorf, 1959). Stedman Jones (2001, p 4) argues that Parsons' usage of Durkheim was flawed and that as a result Durkheim was "damned by the company who sought him out". A view that denies the existence of conflict in society, and even goes so far as to suggest that the market will deliver the correct balance of jobs, all of which are interdependent, is underscored by a largely conservative political position. Despite this, or maybe because of it, functionalism has a significant place in understanding both capitalist society in the 20th century and the development of sociology, which sought to reflect what it observed, since capitalism seems to be remarkably durable.

A sociology of work?

Capitalism, however, does not run smoothly and its development is characterised by periods of 'boom and bust'. Classical economics, as well as Marxist theory, point to the periodic crises within capitalism, which result in periods of low economic growth. Koch (2001) points out that capitalist expansion continues within a complex set of relationships, which are determined both socially and economically, but that these relationships are both constructed and contested by a series of struggles. Aglietta (1987), however, argued that when a number of factors combine, capitalism generates both economic expansion and social cohesion and as such questioned much of the postwar sociological and economic orthodox thinking in relation to capitalist development.

The intention is not to engage in a discussion of both complex and specialised sociological accounts of society, but to introduce a 'sociology of work', which has developed since the Second World War. By now, it will be apparent that an understanding of work, or production, cannot be separated from an understanding of the economic foundation of society. Aglietta focused on the development of postwar economic expansion and stability through his analysis of 'Fordism'. This refers to the organisation of mass production, and economies of scale, typically seen in large-scale manufacturing industry, especially motor car manufacture – hence the term 'Fordism'. Within this organisation, work is highly regulated and controlled – a process termed 'Taylorism'. Fordism, however, also saw the creation of institutionalised mechanisms for dealing with industrial conflict and Aglietta suggests that it also served to create a period of reducing wage differentials and a rise in general prosperity. To think of this in another way, it was a period of long and continued economic growth.

Such large-scale production, with its focus on mainly male employment, has disappeared in most European countries. It has been replaced with a less regulated approach to production and the current period is sometimes called 'post-Fordism'. This has led to a greater emphasis on productivity, less labour market regulation and the creation of more low-paid jobs. This has resulted in increasing numbers of people being in work, yet still poor (Walker and Walker, 1997).

Work as fulfilment and participation

So far we have explored production and work in purely sociological terms, looking at its place in society and how it is organised. The suggestion is that large-scale production and factory-based work is a thing of the past – certainly in Europe – and that the conditions associated with this also belong to another era. Work, in current society, is increasingly seen as something that should bring about personal fulfilment. It is no longer portrayed as a means to an end, but rather as something that is, in itself, an end.

The current era is often referred to as the information society and a third 'industrial revolution' (Castells, 1996). Shapiro and Varian (1999) argue that the development of new technologies, the so-called information technologies, has driven these changes. Bell (1980) suggests that this will influence not only how we access information and knowledge, but also the nature and type of work people do. The nature of work has been changed by the development of new technologies as well as by changing business practices. These things combined have helped fuel the development of the service economy and a feature of this in Europe is the changing pattern of female employment (Esping-Andersen, 2002).

There is a focus on the *quality* of people's working lives, as well as what they do and produce. Social psychologists have gone further to suggest that work provides a source of psychological stability (Jahoda, 1982). It does this by providing structure and purpose to people's daily lives, but also brings them into contact with other people and gives them a clearer sense of identity. Gallie and Russell (1998) show that when people are in regular employment their levels of satisfaction with life in general are higher than those who are workless. Unemployment has a damaging psychological as well as financial effect on people's lives (Warr, 1987, 2002). Work, then, is a source of financial and psychological well-being. In this regard, it becomes central to people's lives and the psychological aspect is increasingly being promoted. This is all part of contemporary work. The hierarchical structure of Taylorist practices, which characterised factory production (Fordism), is giving way to less hierarchical forms of work organisation. Large organisations no longer have personnel but human resources (HR) departments. Beaumont (1993), in a text for HR managers, set out the HR mantra that *individuals* are the key to a successful organisation. Thus, in the world of work, individual need seems to have overtaken collective agreements, arguably making collective organisation more difficult.

Nonetheless, work also provides the potential for social relationships (Argyle, 1991) so the importance of belonging and being involved should not be overlooked. Wall and Lischeron (1977) set out the importance of employees being involved in decision making that affects not only their immediate work environment, but also the company overall. Most importantly, people want job satisfaction – work has to be a psychologically, as well as economically, rewarding activity. Gallie and colleagues (1998) show that technological changes and new forms of management have led to improvements in 'job satisfaction', confirming the link between the new technologies and organisation change.

Activity

Think about the work you do or have done in the past. How was it organised and how did you experience it? To what extent would you call it a rewarding experience?

This brief reflective pause on the nature of your own work could have produced many and varied responses. What needs to be addressed in sociological terms is whether the technological and organisational changes have led to a better quality of work life. Gallie and colleagues (1998) discovered that new organisational and management forms do not affect all employees equally. For staff in management positions and more traditional 'white-collar jobs', the changes have consolidated their benefits: for those in lower-skilled, manual jobs, little has changed.

So, does Castell's third industrial revolution herald a situation that fundamentally changes the nature of work and society and generates a win–win position? Steijn (2004), in a review of the impact of information and communication technology on working lives, explores further the winners and losers in contemporary work. The conclusions echo that of Gallie and colleagues' investigations. Steijn (2004, p 43), citing De Beer (2001), notes that those with fewer educational qualifications are some of the losers in the new economy. There are also risks with the new jobs, such as repetitive strain injury and increased levels of stress, often driven by the demands of specific software. These 'risks' are not evenly spread, with lower-paid administrators being more susceptible (Dhondt and Kraan, 2001, cited in Steijn, 2004, p 43).

Gallie (2002) draws similar conclusions in relation to fulfilment and personal development through employment, arguing that semi- and non-skilled employees (about 40% of all jobs) have jobs of poor labour quality. What begins to emerge quite starkly is that benefits from technology and new ways of working benefit those who are already engaged in 'good' jobs. For the low-skilled and low-paid, the risks and deprivations of work have simply changed their nature.

One further feature of current work organisation is a phenomenon known as 'flexibility'. Many job advertisements require a flexible approach from the prospective applicant; flexibility is increasingly seen as an important quality to bring to work. It suggests a dynamic, even exciting, environment where the employee is met with a range of challenges that will bring about a level of satisfaction. For many people, however, the nature of flexibility is job insecurity. The father of one of the authors worked in the same factory for 40 years, his father at the same steelworks for 50. Growing up in the East Midlands in the 1960s, it was commonplace for young men to be told 'get a job at Rolls Royce (Derby) or the ironworks (Stanton) and you'll have a job for life'. Within 10 years, both organisations had collapsed, leading to high levels of redundancy. The old steelworks, once employing over 10,000, now employs less than 300: there are no longer 'jobs for life'. Thus, flexibility has come to mean the need and ability to learn new skills and to adapt (hence the greater vulnerability of those with lower educational attainment and ability) as well as job insecurity. The latter is greatest among those with low- and non-skilled jobs, yet still significant among professional and managerial staff (Gallie, 2002, p 107). Flexibility is a feature of the current market-driven society, not confined to the working poor, but something that creates uncertainties for all groups of workers.

Classical sociology reclaimed?

Durkheim argued that capitalism and the division of labour offered the potential for personal fulfilment. Applied to contemporary society, it would seem that for capitalism to achieve this for the majority, it still has some way to go. The changing nature of work has brought about new opportunities and possibly created a situation where a greater emphasis is placed on skill acquisition, but in terms of human potential this remains largely untapped.

Marx saw capitalism as being exploitative and destructive of human potential. The changes in work practices and organisation would appear to indicate that the nature of contemporary capitalism has changed on the surface, yet the levels of insecurity and low-skilled jobs identify an alternative explanation. The nature of exploitation has merely changed.

Europe has seen a considerable shift away from large-scale production, with an economy based on new technologies and the service industry, dependent on what people spend just as much as what they produce. Often this has meant only that the site of production has been moved: steel, cars, even clothing is increasingly produced in developing nations (just look at the labels on your own clothes), while Europeans benefit from cheap consumer goods. In a straightforward way, this is a feature of a global economy – a theme that will be developed in Chapter Four – but still a global capitalist economy (Yeates, 2001).

Work can be fulfilling, but for some it always was. What of the operator in a call centre, or the minimum-waged care assistant? How fulfilling is work for them and how far do new management techniques apply? The evidence suggests that while things appear to have changed, beneath the surface the essential relationship has remained. In this sense, we have come full circle and we now turn to one of the original sociological concepts developed by Marx: alienation.

Marx and alienation

The concept of alienation appears in two of Marx's early works, *Economic and Philosophical Manuscripts* of 1844, and *The German Ideology* of 1845-46 (Marx. 1970). Recently, there has been a revival of interest in the concept of alienation (Ferguson and Lavalette, 2004; Mooney, 2004).

Activity

The stages of alienation are described below; think about how these apply both to the nature of work in contemporary society reviewed earlier and to your own experiences.

Alienation from the product refers to the extent to which a person's work or labour is dominated by external forces and factors. These are 'alien' to the worker, that is, they form no part of his or her 'being'. The more effort that is put into working, according to Marx, the greater the extent of the subjugation to work; therefore the worker has less time for themselves, leaving a feeling of being devalued (to use a contemporary concept). Marx argues that under capitalist conditions, work is the means of survival; it is only the means to an end. The worker becomes 'enslaved' for two reasons: first, the nature of the work dominates the worker and, second, without the work there is no longer any means of 'subsistence'. Workers also, for the most part, do not share in the fruits of their labours. For example, builders who construct five-bedroomed houses rarely receive enough in wages to afford to buy one.

The large-scale factory work that characterised the early development of *industrial* capitalism is disappearing in the UK, but it is important to note that in many of the service industries, similar aspects of alienation can be identified. For example, workers in expensive hotels cannot afford to stay in them; staff in mortgage centres often arrange very large mortgages, yet would not be eligible for one themselves; and, of course, workers who produce luxury cars do not earn enough to buy one themselves.

Alienation from the process of labour is a crucial second area and this is inevitably linked to the first stage, alienation from the product. For Marx, work is an external force, and so can rarely bring about fulfilment. Real development of 'mental and physical energy' cannot come about through work, which only brings exhaustion, both physical and mental. Marx, drawing on the work of Hegel, referred to this as 'self-alienation', that is, alienation from the 'self' as opposed to alienation from the 'subject' of work. Consequently:

> ... the worker, therefore, feels himself at home only during his leisure time, whereas at work he feels homeless. His work is not voluntary but imposed, *forced labour*. It is not the satisfaction of a need, but only a means for satisfying other needs. Its alien character is clearly shown by the fact that as soon as there is no physical or other compulsion it is avoided like the plague. (Marx, 1844, reproduced in Jordan, 1972, pp 127-8, emphasis in original)

The rise of the National Lottery is some evidence of people's current desire to avoid work and to find a different way of having their needs met. Frequently, this is not so much related to what people do for work, but rather to the demoralising demands of the organisations that employ them.

Alienation from society is, then, the inevitable consequence of alienated labour. Marx argues that this is also firmly embedded in capitalism – the means of production and exchange. The route by which Marx arrives at this idea begins with an understanding of people and their 'natural' state. People have both physical and 'mental' needs, and Marx argues that labour and work in a capitalist society create the conditions whereby people are alienated from other people. Ultimately, the way people respond to both the products and the processes of work is carried forward into how they respond to others. Put simply, the nature of work is one of exploitation, and this results in alienation; this is then carried into the whole set of societal relationships – people use each other and the collective nature of people becomes disaggregated. As a consequence of the destructive nature of work, social relationships are distorted and broken.

In *The German Ideology* Marx (1970) clarifies the sociological nature of alienation as being a direct result of the nature of production. For him, it followed that the owner of the means of production was the ultimate source of alienation, that is, the bourgeois *class*. In his later work, he used the term 'estrangement' to refer to 'self-alienation', but reiterated his view that alienation could only be overcome by changing the nature of social relationships, which are premised on people's exploited labour. In short, while the economy is organised in the interests of capital, alienation will be inevitable. Thus, Marx argues that the relationship between people and work is one of exploitation and this is the defining feature of capitalist society.

Fromm and 'the sane society'

The concept of alienation, which began in Marx's analysis of capitalism, has come to acquire a different set of meanings. Is it located in society's economic organisation or is it predominantly a mental or emotional concept? The term has been used in many ways and has come to mean a little more than a general feeling of malaise. Erich Fromm's (2002) book, *The Sane Society*, first published in 1955, explores the concept in a different way.

Fromm was a member of the Frankfurt School of sociologists, whose thinking attempted a fusion of the ideas of Marx and Freud. He developed the concept of alienation in a different manner. He suggests that the two key concepts for understanding current capitalist society are quantification and abstraction. The former refers to how the capitalist seeks to give everything a value. Fromm illustrates this when he states that we talk about a 'three-million-dollar bridge' or a 'twenty-cent cigar' (2002, p 111). Later, he argues that often we deal with the human condition in an abstract way. An example he gives is that of a headline proclaiming 'Shoe manufacturer dies', when in reality a man who owned and managed a factory in which other people manufactured shoes has died. The man's human qualities, his 'hopes and frustrations', are reduced to the 'abstract formula of economic function'. To this extent, Fromm's use of the concept has clear resonances with Marx. He continues, however, to give alienation a very clear and unambiguous mental, psychological and spiritual nature by connecting it with 'idolatry'. He concludes that ultimately alienation becomes a force that generates insanity, when people lose contact with their sense of self, "distorted by the unconscious forces which operate *in them*" (2002, pp 113-20, emphasis added). Marx identified alienation from the self as a consequence of material conditions; Fromm leaves them behind. So, alienation is no longer located within the means of production, but is a psychological concept, whose roots may lie in society but whose answers lie in the 'self' rather than the material conditions of work and society.

Later Fromm argues that the limitations of Marx lie in the exclusive emphasis on economic relationships. For Fromm, Marx's focus on achieving liberation through a mainly economic route results in an avoidance of people's essential human nature. It is here, however, that Fromm reveals his own position and the Freudian overtones inherent in his work. While Marx had an essentially optimistic view of humankind, and saw people as being destroyed by the nature of capitalism, Fromm sees humankind in essentially negative terms, characterised by a desire for power and (self-)destruction. Ultimately for Fromm, alienation becomes synonymous with all the evils (real or imagined) of industrial capitalism. In this way, it loses its Marxist meaning and is transformed into something else.

Marx and the disappearance of alienation

As a postscript, it is worth thinking about how the term alienation disappeared. Jordan (1972) offers two possible explanations for this. First, he argues that for Marx the means of production is the cause of alienation; therefore, alienation can only be dealt with by a revolutionary change in economic relationships. Thus, it follows that the concept can be subsumed into the class struggle. Since

Marx's later works concerned the nature of the class struggle and a scientific investigation of the economic basis of capitalism, there was no longer a need to develop the concept further; it is part and parcel of the nature of capitalist society. Second, he suggests, from a reading of *Capital Volume III*, that Marx came to see *self-alienation* (or estrangement) as an "unavoidable consequence of the necessity to work" (Jordan, 1972, p 19). Whatever the mode of production, there will always be some necessity to work; therefore, some alienation will be inevitable.

The crux of Marx's work is that alienation is a *material* reality and for this reason it is located within the process of production and not within the 'self'. Fromm attempts this fusion, but the location of alienation in *production* renders this fusion pointless. It is the nature of work and the relationships that result from it that create self-alienation, and aspects of this will be explored later in the book in relation to consumption.

By focusing on production and work, we discover the basis for poverty and the resulting social exclusion. Low wages are paid, not because of people's lack of skills or the usefulness of their labour, but rather as part of a market mechanism that seeks to preserve class interests and exploit labour. Poverty is generated either by low-paid work or no work, both conditions being determined by the exploitative nature of contemporary society. So, as Byrne (2002) noted in his discussion of social exclusion, exploitation matters.

Note

[1] Durkheim's work has undergone substantial revision since it was seen as the sociological straw man in the 1960s and 1970s. An influential work is Stedman Jones' excellent and thought-provoking rehabilitation of Durkheim as a socialist and radical thinker. The summaries of Durkheim here owe much to this work (Stedman Jones, 2001), as well as to previous summaries in Giddens (1978).

FOUR

Work, exclusion, poverty and social work

This chapter will explore how the concept of production and work can be applied to social work practice. It will look at how work (or the lack of it) impacts on family life and how this can generate the problems encountered by social workers. It will also explore the relationship between perceived 'social problems' and production. The chapter will conclude with an analysis of social work as 'production'.

Production, poverty and family life

A traditional view of family life and work is that the family provides the (usually male) worker with a 'safe haven'. This is explored in the next section, which looks at how society 'reproduces itself'. Our concern here is to show the relevance of theories of work and production for social workers. The sociology may not appear to be immediately relevant; however, it is through understanding the nature of production that we can develop a better understanding of poverty, social exclusion and inequality.

One of the aims of this book is to show how sociological explanations of exclusion and poverty are of relevance to social work practice. Whether or not people 'work' the level of their wages, or income, is a significant factor in their social position. The majority of people who use social work services are likely to be poor, either through not working or through being employed in a low- or even minimum-waged job. Jones (2001) argues that poverty is still a major factor for the majority of service users. Theories of production explain that capitalism seeks to drive down wages. Thus, poverty is endemic within the economic system and any understanding of it needs to begin here. Put more clearly, poverty is a result of low-paid employment and worklessness; these are created and sustained by the economic system. In taking this position, we explicitly reject those explanations of poverty that locate it in individual failings (Murray, 1984, 1990, 1994). Murray developed the idea of an 'underclass' of poor people, created by unemployment and the welfare state which encourages them to remain out of work. For Murray, poverty is located very clearly within personal failings and 'fecklessness' – a word much used by some Victorian groups when describing the poor. In social policy terms, it is often associated with a distinction between the 'deserving' and 'undeserving' poor. So, when working with families who are experiencing poverty, social workers in the early 21st century face the same tension as did the early social workers: individual or structural failings?

Poverty and children

The Department of Health's guidance for comprehensive assessments of children in need and at risk begins with stating the level of child poverty:

> There are approximately 11 million children in England. It is estimated that over 4 million of them are living in families with less than half the average household income.... Over the last generation, this has become a divided country. While most areas have benefited from rising living standards, the poorest neighbourhoods have tended to become more run down, more prone to crime, more cut off from the labour market. (DH, 2000, p 1)

Many social workers are involved with providing services to children and their families, usually because of 'risk factors'. There is a perception of poor people that results in greater levels of surveillance by social work and other agencies (see Garrett, 2004, for a recent example). The relationship between poverty and child abuse is complex, and it would appear that this is more prevalent among poorer people, but the level of surveillance is greater. Another factor is the impact of poverty in generating isolation and stress, both of which are seen to be significant factors in increasing the likelihood of child maltreatment (Swift, 1995; Winter and Connolly, 2005). There is, perhaps, a danger that too simplistic a correlation between poverty and abuse can be drawn and factors are many and varied (Corby, 1993; McSherry, 2004). At least one author has suggested that in countries where relative poverty is reduced (for example, Sweden) and where there are high levels of social cohesion (for example, Scandinavian states and southern European countries), child deaths (if not actual abuse) are lower than in the UK (Beckett, 2005).

The focus here is not on child abuse, but on the important aspects of poverty and worklessness that social workers should be utilising when undertaking assessments and interventions with families who experience levels of social exclusion and relative poverty.

In the UK, there has been a focus since 1997 on reducing child poverty, with key measures being to encourage parents into work and support low wages with increased levels of state benefit (Hills and Stewart, 2005; Pantazis et al, 2006). Indeed, the commitment to ending child poverty has become one of apparent all-party consensus (Cameron, 2006; Letwin, 2006), although differences in how this can be achieved remain. The extent of child poverty in 1996 was considerable, and it is important to note that this followed the introduction of 'neoliberal' economic policies by the Conservative government from 1979 onwards. That is, there was a systematic withdrawal from policies that promoted equality.

Gregg and colleagues (1999) demonstrate the link between child poverty and worklessness. They noted that over half of children who were poor lived in a household were there was no working adult. Twenty per cent of all poor children in workless households lived with two parents, while 34% lived with one. They also noted that lone-parent households were significantly more likely to be workless (42% of lone parents in work) than two-parent households. They accept that the rise in numbers of lone parents accounts for around 20% of the rise in child poverty; however, the most significant factor is the changing rates of employment among all families. Thus, it is the nature of changes in production – employment opportunities and levels of wages – that has generated child poverty.

The Child Poverty Action Group is an important organisation that collects data and campaigns for the end of child poverty. Figures from 2000 indicated that while 62% of all lone parents lived in poverty, by far the largest group of poor children lived with couples – a total of almost five million people, with women and children more likely to experience persistently low incomes than men. The highest proportion of children in poverty in the UK lived in Wales. This also connects with the demise of production. South Wales, which includes some of the most deprived areas in the whole of Europe, has seen considerable rises in unemployment, with closures of the mining and steel industries (David and Blewitt, 2003).

The importance of poverty for social workers becomes even more pressing when considering the impacts it has on children. These are well documented (CPAG, 2000; Vleminckx and Smeeding, 2001; Esping-Andersen, 2002) and show how all aspects of children's life chances are adversely affected by poverty. To begin with, they are less likely to survive birth, and subsequent death rates are higher than in professional classes. As they get older, they will have poorer school attendance records and record lower levels of educational attainment. Throughout their lives they are at greater risk of accidents, will experience a poorer diet and in teenage years be at greater risk of involvement in criminal activity or of being sexually exploited.

The Acheson Report (1998) shows that children who live in lower socioeconomic groups are more likely to have diet deficiencies; the extent of this difference in diet has increased since 1990. The birth weights of children born into the lowest socioeconomic groups are lower than those of wealthier mothers. While this maybe attributable to poorer diet and higher rates of smoking, the difference between birth weights as determined by socioeconomic groups *increased* in the 10 years before the report, despite an overall *decrease* in the numbers of mothers smoking. Thus, personal 'failings' cannot be held to be the sole cause of the phenomenon – and, even if this were the case, which factors generate the 'need' for smoking, drug use and the consumption of comfort foods? The authors of this book suggest, perhaps predictably, that the main factor is poverty.

Finally, how do children themselves experience poverty? Ridge's wide-ranging study (2002) of child poverty covered all areas of their lives, from access to material resources, social integration, family life and school. There is a high level of resilience:

> "I wouldn't bother [asking for something expensive] I don't see the point because if we haven't got very much money then we can't get it so I don't mind" (Martin, 11, two-parent family). (Ridge, 2002, p 98)

Nonetheless, such resilience often had a personal cost, as Nell (17, two-parent family) describes in relation to free school meals:

> "I don't because I realised when I was in year 7 that the people who got free school meals were teased ... I couldn't handle that as I was already getting teased enough so I don't get free school meals." (Ridge, 2002, p 82)

Children's voices are often not heard, and the latter account provides evidence of how even progressive policies can often leave children suffering because of poverty. Thus, when the concept of production is expanded to include those who do not work, the impact for those engaged in working with families is clear.

The critical decision for social work is how such factors will be addressed and dealt with in both intervention and assessment. This brings us back to the enduring tensions within social work: individual faults or structural factors and the extent of social work's engagement with the political process and developing a collective strategy.

Production and 'race'

There is a solid recent history of social work engaging with black and minority ethnic (BME) groups, who experience for the most part both exclusion and relative poverty (Cheetham, 1972; Husband, 1995; Lewis G., 2000). 'Race', in itself, is a highly contested term (Penketh and Ali, 1997), with a history connected to the discredited quasi-scientific theories of eugenics that found their extreme expression in the politics of Hitler's fascism. These focused on the extermination not only of non-Aryan groups (Jews and gypsies being the most notable), but also of groups of people who were regarded as 'subhuman' and this included disabled as well as gay and lesbian people. They suggest that the concept of 'race' can be said to describe the exploitation, marginalisation and exclusion of people based on actual or perceived differences.

Skin colour is the most obvious difference, although religion also features large, for example, the Northern Irish 'Troubles' and 'Islamophobia'. The term 'racism' is used to refer to the systematic disadvantaging of and discrimination against one group by another more powerful group and a definition that was adopted in the 1980s goes beyond mere prejudice. It suggests that when racial prejudice is accompanied by institutional or personal power, racism results (Eberhardt and Fiske, 1998).

In the UK and many other Western countries, the processes of 'race' have been linked to colonialism. Hall (1992) and Gilroy (1987) linked the concept of 'race' to the process of systematic discrimination throughout colonial history. The history of colonialism was based on the economic exploitation of resources, both physical and human. In a specifically UK context, this would include involvement in the slave trade, which provided not only some individual traders with considerable wealth, but also whole cities, such as Liverpool and Bristol. It would include the colonisation of land, notably on the Indian subcontinent and Africa.

The process of migration into postwar Britain can be termed colonisation in reverse, with the net result being further economic and social exploitation of a particular group. The whole process of migration tends to provide net gains for the host country while placing each subsequent group of migrant workers at the lower end of the socioeconomic scale (Castles and Kosac, 1972). Thus, this particular analysis of race emphasises the relationship between racism and economic exploitation; it is located within the realm of 'production'. Black and minority ethnic groups are *more likely* to be found in lower socioeconomic groups than white people (Palmer et al, 2005). However, over 90% of the poor are white (Palmer et al, 2005).

Thus, an analysis of the statistical data confirms that BME groups both experience higher levels of unemployment and poverty and are more likely to have lower-paid jobs (Palmer et al, 2005). It is also the case that 70% of the BME population live in the 88 most deprived local authority districts (SEU, 2004b). In relation to housing, the same report provided evidence that this is greatest for Pakistani and Bangladeshi families. Garvie (2001), in a report for Shelter, a charity for homeless people, investigated the living conditions of asylum seekers and found that 20% of those in privately rented accommodation were living in conditions that were unfit for human habitation. Therefore, while BME people experience all forms of discrimination, this is located within production, since the other conditions, such as poor housing, follow from the general low level of wages. The economic forces that underlie racism have long been overlooked by social work in the pursuit of its diversity agenda (Garret, 2002), which has emphasised individual attitudes and responses to 'race', 'ethnicity' and 'difference', albeit within racist structures (Dominelli, 1988, 1997). More recently, Izumi (2005) has argued for a more personalised approach to understanding power relations, criticising what he viewed as a weakness of this conventional approach. There is nothing inherently 'wrong' with such an approach: social workers need to explore their own attitudes towards different ethnic groups, for example.

However, focusing on this area alone does not necessarily lead to widespread improvements for people. The experiences of exclusion of Asian young people, much reported in the UK media, are located within production and the failure of government to ensure their need for work is met (Richards, 2006; Temko, 2006). Their experience of deprivation, exclusion and poverty has much in common with that of white people in similar circumstances (Evans, 2006). It is therefore not difficult to begin to argue that 'race' is a concept that can be used to set poor people against each other. A focus on difference, rather than what people have and experience in common, could serve to perpetuate inequality, rather than address it, precisely because it does not deal with the actual causes of the inequality. A divided working class can, in a Marxist analysis, only benefit capital.

The effects of production: mental ill health

One of the most well-known pieces of Durkheim's sociological investigation is into suicide (Durkheim, 2002). While others have taken issue with his methodology and conclusions (Stedman Jones, 2001), the work confirms the relationship between aspects of mental ill health and social organisation. Durkheim postulated that there are different types of suicide and that a particular form is that which he termed 'anomic'. This is where the individual feels isolated from and by society and Durkheim argued that this increased in times of social uncertainty. The importance for us is that Durkheim took an action that could be said to be inextricably bound up with individuals and their personal sets of circumstances, and sought to explain how this was influenced by social factors. Its significance lies in that not only is it a sociological account, and as such establishes a link between social structures and personal actions, but it also forces an engagement with the organisation of society that generates these anomic feelings.

While Durkheim focused on suicide, potentially a consequence of mental ill health, there is much recent work that highlights the effects of class and racism in relation to mental ill health. It is again important to remember that structural factors are not the sole cause of mental ill health and that in some instances the causes can be located elsewhere. For example, the NHS Health Advisory Service (1995) highlighted the importance of family-based risk factors, especially for child and adolescent mental ill health, yet it also pointed to the combination of social disadvantage and discrimination as being significant. Lloyd (1993, 1998) argued that social inequalities, including class and racism, were significant factors in mental illness, building on a theme developed through the 1990s. It is the interaction of poverty and ethnicity that is to be considered by social workers and those dealing with mental illness, thus shifting the focus of attention away from the individual towards society, and most importantly, perhaps, towards factors of capitalist organisation that lead to unemployment, low wages and poverty

(Beliappa, 1991; Nazroo, 1997). Nazroo (1998) in a subsequent study underlines this in relation to mental ill health and concludes that material factors are of significant relevance, especially for BME groups. Macintyre and colleagues (1993) had earlier pointed to what they termed the ecological effects in relation to mental health, arguing that environmental factors have an impact over and above any sets of personal factors.

Senior and Bhopal (1994) also provide a warning, when using ethnicity as an indicator of mental illness. By focusing on ethnicity, they argue, there is a risk that the focus of intervention becomes BME groups, rather than the material conditions they live under. In this way, the victim is blamed, and the consequence is a further continuation of individualised interventions, dislocated from the material conditions of society.

There is also a strong general correlation between class and mental illness (Weich and Lewis, 1998). It is also important to restate something that may appear to be self-evident: poor housing, unemployment and poverty are all located within an economic system that is based on forms of economic exploitation. So, while many forms of therapeutic intervention focus on individuals, it is important for those involved to be able to ensure that structural factors are not overlooked. Of course, this is not to argue for the absence of individual treatments and therapies. The concern is to place structural inequalities on the agenda, and social workers are in a strong position to do this. The challenge for social workers is to incorporate this into their assessments and interventions and work out ways of engaging in processes to bring about structural as well as personal changes.

It is also important to acknowledge that work itself is an act of production and can be a cause of mental ill health. Workplace-based stress is increasing (Bunting, 2005; Carvel 2006) and this seems to be even more so among professional groups (Jones, 2001 identifies increased stress among social workers). New technologies (see Chapter Three) have created their own health problems. In economies based on large-scale production, there are high risks of physical injury and death related with jobs such as mining, working on the railways and construction. New technologies have to a large extent ended these but shifted attention to workplace stress and other forms of injury, such as repetitive strain injury and illnesses related to poor posture when sitting at computer terminals. In the service sector, abuse from customers is increasing, as signs in many public places evidence. For example, rail commuters are reminded that staff who work on the services they use are frequently subjected to abuse from customers. This may take the form of either physical assault or verbal abuse. In addition, people who do suffer from mental ill health are more likely to be sacked and are more likely to be forced into resignation (SEU, 2004c).

In an important study, Faragher and colleagues (2005) found that stress levels were directly linked to poor job satisfaction, and that this was an important factor in the health (physical and mental) of employees. They identify an increase in automated work processes, which reduce employees' control over workload.

This, combined with temporary employment, associated with outsourcing and short-term contracts, increases job insecurity, while creating a culture of working long hours for those in employment. These factors combine to increase stress and reduce job satisfaction. The study concluded that workers with low levels of job satisfaction are more likely to have reductions in self-esteem and higher levels of anxiety and depression, which ultimately impact on family relationships. In short, poor working conditions impact beyond the workplace. Thus, it would appear that current working practices have merely created new ways to alienate people from their work, which leads to an alienation from the self. The importance of understanding the nature of production becomes clearer.

Production and disability

Disabled people are frequently excluded from aspects of production and work. In the European Union (EU) and the US, despite many pieces of legislation making discrimination illegal, it is still the case that disabled people are more likely to be out of work than members of the able-bodied population (Oliver, 1990; Turning Point, 2004). Other aspects of social organisation also combine to increase the exclusion of disabled people, and an obvious example of this is access to public places and transport (Oliver, 1990). The disability rights movement has been active in placing issues of work and access on the policy agenda, and it could be argued that there has been some success (Oliver, 1990; Shakespeare, 1993; Beresford and Croft, 2004). Social work often focuses on questions of 'attitudes' towards disability. This is indeed important for the social worker–service user relationship, although, as in all areas of social work, it can effectively mask the deeply embedded social and economic nature of the difficulties faced.

The exclusion of wheelchair users relates mainly to issues of access, and this can be addressed by changing access arrangements in workplaces and public spaces. Nevertheless, the incidence of poverty among disabled people is higher than in the able-bodied population (Barnes and Baldwin, 1999; Burchardt, 2000b, 2003), and exclusion from work is central to exclusion in other areas. For learning disabled people, the position is more complex, and they are often overlooked when considering aspects of disability discrimination (Turning Point, 2004, p 3).

Changes in the nature of production and social organisation have removed learning disabled people from the workplace and left them dependent on various forms of benefit and the care of family and social care workers. This exclusion is closely linked to the rise of capitalism, which saw greater regulation and control of the working day and task. Concerns about the fitness of the population combined with this to generate policies of segregation, so at the time that the factory system was becoming dominant, learning disabled people were frequently being placed in workhouses or subnormality hospitals. Because they were 'unproductive', they experienced physical exclusion from society (Ryan with Thomas, 1987).

Within contemporary society, the position of learning disabled people has arguably improved considerably, with moves towards community integration. However, their exclusion from employment seems to have increased, largely as a result of the shift towards a skills-based economy. The job opportunities that are available are few and low-paid, although there are some notable successes, with a leading charity, the Shaw Trust, being concerned solely with finding jobs for disabled people. Even menial jobs, the growth area in the UK, often demand skill levels that can exclude learning disabled people. Nine out of 10 people with a learning disability have no connection with the labour market and those that do are in low-paid employment (Turning Point, 2004), yet even here, people with learning disabilities are often discriminated against illegally. Taylor and colleagues (2005) reported one case where a young man was being paid 29 pence an hour. With economic inclusion effectively blocked, levels of social exclusion increase. The Turning Point report suggests that for many people with learning disabilities there is not even any consideration given to work or meaningful day centre activities:

> For many the typical childhood question 'what will you be when you grow up?' is never asked. This means that there is no climate of expectation to work or aspiration of paid employment, something most of us take for granted. This compounds the lack of life chances open to them through childhood and their adult lives. (Turning Point, 2004, p 11)

While personal attitudes are important, the real key to inclusion is employment, which brings with it not only a degree of financial independence, but also feelings of self-worth and self-esteem. Thus, we can see how the tensions around work highlighted in Chapter Three are brought together. Certainly, work is exploitative, but it also gives a feeling of belonging and worth. It is important to recall that Durkheim saw this as being the case: Marx's concern was not with work per se but rather the nature of exploitation of labour by capital. For learning disabled people, exclusion and isolation is compounded by their exclusion from even the lowest-paid end of the labour market.

Production and age

The relationship between older people and production is changing, largely because of the ageing population in the West, notably within the EU. There are a number of questions here, and while social workers are primarily involved with older people who are in need of 'care', the general relationship between age and work needs to be understood and applied. Older age is associated with poverty (JRF,

2005) but it is also the case that some older people experience high living standards. Walker and Maltby (1997, p 44) point out that "as many other commentators have noted financial and economic security in old age are primarily a function of the interaction of the socio–economic status individuals occupy during their working lives and the pension system". The pension system in most countries also has a strong gender bias and as a consequence women are more likely to experience poverty in their old age than men (Bury, 1995; Dooghe and Appleton, 1995). As a result, older women are among the most socially excluded adults in the EU (Walker and Maltby, 1997). To put this more explicitly, levels of income in older age will be determined mainly by levels of income during the working life, so production matters. Where social care provision is needed in the form of residential care, the nature of the care will often depend on the extent of finances available, and for women, this will more often than not depend on their former husband's/partner's income.

Although poverty is closely linked to ageing, Walker and Maltby (1997, p 55) note that, drawing on the evidence of the 'Eurobarometer', most older people regard themselves as financially secure, even though the most common assessment of their financial situation is one of 'getting by with care'. Recent developments in public policy, however, have begun to examine the prospect of people working longer, as a response to the ageing population. To some extent, this represents a move away from postwar trends in the UK that saw far fewer older people being economically active from the age of 55 upwards, and the early exit policies of the 1980s (Guillemard, 1993). Even allowing for policy shifts, the position of older workers is more vulnerable than that of younger workers; they are more likely to be made redundant, less likely to be promoted and, of course, less likely to be employed (Elchardus and Cohen, 2004).

The difficulties faced by older people in relation to income are a major factor in quality of life in older age for those who remain generally fit and healthy, and, as we have seen, this is also a significant factor when considering residential care provision. Thus, the importance of production for social workers in their contact with service users should by now be clear: it is a major factor in understanding their lives and experiences.

Social work as 'work'

This chapter shows how an understanding of production and work is crucial to gaining sociological insights into the lives of service users. Work, the lack of it and low wages are all determined by the process of production and this impacts on the lives people are able to live. Social workers are faced with the enduring dilemmas thrown up by the analysis of production. Do they focus on individual explanations or structural ones? This is part of the dialectical situation social workers find themselves in. Of course, they will deal with the individual as they are faced with the human consequences of the impact of structural factors. This does not adequately resolve the tension, and social workers have to make choices about the extent to which they are willing to engage in a political process. To follow the sociology of either Marx or Durkheim is akin to taking a political position, either in relation to the Marxist pursuit of an alternative economic system or to Durkheim's belief in 'fairness', and in a democracy it is likely that both could result in reforming policies.

This chapter concludes by turning its attention towards social work as 'work'. It is all well and good to debate what it is that social workers should do, yet the conditions that social workers operate under need to be part of this equation. Much of the recent literature in relation to social work calls it a 'profession' and sees it as being concerned with the provision of services for 'service users', as the General Social Care Council argued in September 2006:

> Social workers and social care workers are expert in helping to facilitate a joined up approach to service provision that benefits services users and the community. (General Social Care Council, 2006, www.gscc.org.uk, emphasis added)

In a study of motivational factors for social work students, the authors found increasing signs that entrants to social work are attracted to it as a well-paid career choice for people who want to make a difference (Price and Simpson, 2004). The reality of current social work is described by Jones (2001), who interviewed experienced frontline staff. He found high levels of job dissatisfaction; working practices and organisation that reduced autonomy; and large amounts of time being taken up with office-based paperwork. This confirms the early work of Dominelli and Hoogveldt (1996), who identified what they termed the 'technocratisation' of social work and attributed this to managerialist tendencies within the public services linked to an analysis of globalisation (see also Khan and Dominelli, 2000, and Webb, 2003, for a discussion of social work and globalisation). Social work is increasingly being organised along 'Taylorist' principles (see Chapter Three), with reductions in the levels of autonomy experienced by social workers. In this way social work is becoming more like a 'job' and less like a profession. To use a sociological term, it is being 'proletarianised'; that is, the people who undertake the work are organised along the same lines as factory workers. We saw in Chapter Three that such trends had been identified by Marx (Gough, 1978) and so it would not be unreasonable to conclude that social workers are likely to experience alienation from their work. Indeed, the work undertaken by Faragher and colleagues (2005) in relation to workplace stress could easily be applied to social workers.

An evaluation of the common assessment framework in the UK for children's services revealed an increase in workloads that most respondents thought was poorly supported (Taylor, 2006). Stress and physical ailments are common among social care staff. A survey of days lost in local government in 2003/04 showed that while the average social worker was absent through illness for 13 working days, domiciliary care staff had the highest absenteeism rate of 21 days (Heyes, 2005).

In a developed service economy, the importance of Marx's second phase of alienation becomes clearer. The process of labour now dominates sectors of employment that previously allowed for greater worker autonomy and freedom. Nowhere is this truer than in the so-called 'semi-professions' such as teaching and social work, which interestingly have also been referred to as proletarian professions following Poulantzas (1978). Teachers and social workers are employed by someone else and while there are certain aspects of their work that are under their control, the processes are increasingly driven by external forces. Social workers have their work regulated by substantial policy and procedure documents, both local and national. These govern the way in which interventions are undertaken, that is, the process of labour. Attached to this are ever-increasing regulation and control mechanisms, not of the product, but of the process of work. The activity of doing social work ceases to belong to the worker.

The Case Con manifesto of the 1970s contained this paragraph:

> All social workers should join NALGO where possible, since this is the union that actually negotiates on behalf of most social workers. But obviously other organizations, such as NAPO for probation officers, will be more appropriate to some Case Con supporters. Social workers can make the union more democratic at a local level by setting up departmental committees and forging them into shop stewards' committees. But the fight for democratic control on any other level requires linking up with other militants. This should be done by joining or setting up a local NALGO action group, or NAPO members' action group, and drawing on the experience of other militants through a national organization. Links should be forged with other rank-and-file groups (e.g. Rank-and-File Teachers, the Hospital Worker, Nurses Action Group), militant tenants groups and squatters. (Case Con Manifesto, www.radical.org.uk/barefoot/casecon.htm)

What this radical manifesto did was to locate social workers as *workers* within society and argued that they should form alliances with other groups. Joyce and colleagues (1988) attempted to develop this into a late 1980s' context – important, since this was at a time when the Conservative Party in the UK pursued neoliberal economic policies and mounted a sustained attack on local government. They concluded that strike action may sometimes be necessary, but argued that social workers and their trades union (at that time NALGO) should seek broader alliances not just with other workers, but also the general public (1988, p 284).

A cursory review of the social work press news columns since 2004 shows that social workers rarely engage in industrial action. Therefore when they do, it is all the more noticeable. They are frequently charged with putting vulnerable people at risk, and this acts as a bulwark against action. Nevertheless, social workers have threatened or taken action in relation to pay and conditions in Aberdeen (September 2005), Derbyshire (June 2004), Hull and Dorset (July 2004), Lincolnshire (April 2005), Nottingham (February 2004) and Swansea (October 2005). One of the longest disputes was in Liverpool, where the cause was not pay but staff shortages and the resulting heavy workloads as well as changes to procedures that in the workers' view placed vulnerable children at increased levels of risk. The suspension of staff for their conduct in the dispute led to further action (February 2005). In a comment on this, Beresford (2004) argued for social workers to enter into alliances with service users to expose some of the poor working conditions of social care staff. He encouraged them to involve service users networks in their campaigns, arguing that many service users value the work undertaken by social workers and are able to distinguish this from the nature of the organisation they work for. It is also the case that the different strike actions were all treated, even by the social work press, as localised disputes, yet they were of national importance, and no attempt was made to make wider connections between them.

Production theories should therefore be something that social workers apply to their own employment. In this regard, they are subject to the same exploitative economic systems that increase 'surplus value'. Of course, social work salaries are not low, but, as we demonstrated in Chapter Three, the relationship to the means of production is not determined by wage levels but rather by who controls the work. In this way, social care workers need to recognise their own position in the economy and processes of production in 21st-century society.

Part Three
Reproduction

Theoretical concepts: family,
and discour

This chapter explores the core concept of reproduction in sociological theory and analyses gender and family relationships as functional to the reproduction of capital. The contribution of feminism is considered, especially in relation to women's paid and unpaid work. The chapter concludes with an exploration of 'discourse' as reproduction.

What do we mean by reproduction?

Within sociology, reproduction refers to the mechanisms by which society creates, maintains and recreates the conditions for it to continue. So, while production concerns itself with work and how society organises itself to produce goods and wealth, reproduction is concerned with how society organises the lives of its population to ensure that they participate in 'production'. Classical Marxist theory, therefore, explores how capitalism organises itself to ensure that capitalism continues to thrive and how the state takes on the role of organising society to this end.

Reproduction also has come to be closely related to the sociology of the family. Sociologists have developed different perspectives on this, but the primary concern here is to examine functionalist and feminist critiques of it from the 1970s onwards.

Finally, in more recent developments, aspects of sociology have focused on discourse. This is mainly associated with developments out of Marxism by Foucault, and has become one of the dominant sociological developments of the past 15 years.

Reproducing capitalism

Activity

Think about your own interactions with organisations/institutions that dominate your life. What are they? How do they affect you?

We all have contact with a number of different organisations during the course of our daily lives. These organisations give a structure to how we see and experience the world and they all work on the premise that the kind of social relationships they generate are 'normal'. Families are one of the most obvious sites of reproduction, both in the literal sense of the term and in the sociological sense. Within families the process of socialisation serves to prepare children – the next generation of workers – for their place within society. As Corrigan and Leonard (1978, pp 75-6) state:

> It is not enough to have hundreds of young workers who all refuse to work under capitalist production, or who feel that they have the right to control capital…. They must think like workers in a capitalist society; they must see that the major social relationships of that society are not ones that they can have any control over.

A good example of this process is the education system, which prepares people for their place within society. Willis (1978) argues that the system of education was intended to produce sufficient workers in the various sectors and that schools also ensured a disciplined workforce. Almost 30 years later how accurate is this? There is little doubt that the widening participation agenda for higher education in the UK has resulted in far more working-class students – referred to as 'non-traditional entrants', an epithet that in itself highlights the class divide within higher education. However, two factors are beginning to emerge. First, the evidence remains strong that social class is the biggest single determining factor in relation to educational outcomes – even allowing for widening access to higher education (Reay et al, 2005). Thus, whatever changes may have been made, class still matters. Second, there is growing evidence that the salaries and wages of graduates, especially those from the post-1992 universities, are not as high as they used to be and it is probable that students from non-traditional backgrounds are the ones more likely to enter employment sectors with lower graduate pay (O'Leary and Sloane, 2005). This is another example of the dialectic: the appearance is of greater participation, which masks the reality of continuing class divisions.

The essential argument is that the nature of social relationships reflects the nature of a capitalist society and these relationships set the limits of what we come to see as commonplace and accepted.

The family and reproduction

Activity

Think about your experiences of family life. What type of family did you live in? Was this any different to that of your parents or grandparents? How have changes to work affected your experiences of family life?

Family life is one of those areas that all of us have some experience of – even if it is the absence of it. It conjures up a cosy image, even though the reality for many people is different. With your experiences of family in mind, we will now explore the sociology around it.

Engels' (1968) analysis of family and marriage is one of the first attempts to expose the nature of personal relationships and how these can be constructed in ways that serve vested interests. Historically, for the bourgeois, the family was the arena through which male property rights would be passed on through the generations, while the working classes were reduced to using their children as labour, in effect engaging in their exploitation as part of an economic family unit. In the developed world, such exploitation no longer exists in this form, although the extent of child labour in the production of goods that the developed world consumes is well documented (ILO: The Director General, 2006). Nevertheless, the family, which is seen as one of the most enduring and universal forms of human organisation, is central to the sociology of reproduction.

Parsons (1954) and Parsons and Bale (1955) suggested that the family as a unit is functional to the smooth organisation of capitalism and that the *nuclear* family developed as a response to industrial society. The nuclear family is usually defined as a married, heterosexual couple, living in one household with their children (Allan and Crow, 2001). The functionalist argument is that prior to industrialisation, families in a given household were frequently multi-generational and that the economic organisation of society encouraged this. So, a peasant family would benefit from all members being engaged in some form of work to provide an adequate subsistence level. A wealthier family would provide for a number of generations, and for that matter servants, under the same roof. Social mobility – that is, the capacity to move up the social scale (or even down it) – was low and actual mobility – the need or desire to leave your place of birth to find work – was also low. In fact, in the UK, the 1601 Poor Law established the principle that parishes provided help to the poor of *their own parish*, reflecting the static nature of society (Englander, 1998).

The process of industrialisation led to a movement of people from the land (countryside) to the city in search of work. Parsons argues that this was the beginning of the mobile family that could move around the country in search of employment, something that the industrial system both enabled and encouraged. A family with more than two generations would therefore have their mobility substantially reduced; hence Parsons' claim that it was the economic and social organisation of industrial capital that led to the primacy of the nuclear family. In the UK in the 1980s, when there were high levels of unemployment, a high-ranking cabinet minister, Norman Tebbit, exhorted the unemployed to follow his father's example and 'get on their bikes' to look for work. The intention was to encourage people, mainly in the areas hardest hit by unemployment (the North of England, Scotland and Wales), to move to areas where there were more jobs. This could not be easily achieved, however, and all the more so if the move involved multi-generations.

The division of labour within the home usually associated with the nuclear family is one where the man is engaged in paid employment outside the home, with the woman servicing a range of family-based needs: bearing and caring for children, and providing daily care in terms of cooking, cleaning and generally running the home.

Parsons' views of the family have received much criticism. One area of criticism is that history does not readily support his claim. Laslett and Wall (1972) investigated family forms prior to industrialisation in the UK and discovered that the nuclear family was commonplace. Young and Willmott (1957), in their study of the postwar East End of London, discovered an extensive network of family and kinship, with relatively little actual or social mobility, with families living in either multi-generational households or with parents and grandparents living close by.

A second area of criticism comes from Marxists. This book began with the exploitation of the family and how it becomes subject to the economic demands of society. On one level, Marxists could agree with the functionalist claim that the nuclear family serves the interests of capital. Where Marxists differ is that they would not see the family as 'natural' or 'functional' but as representing a mechanism for control in the interests of a dominant economic class. The expectation is for the wage earner to be focused on providing for his or her family. This acts as a mechanism to control and regulate work (production) and to discipline the workforce, rendering it less likely to engage in action to improve its position. Thus, Marxists have often seen the family as a source of what they term 'false consciousness', implying that it prevents the providers from seeing the true nature of social relationships and the subjugation of a largely male workforce (Zaretsky, 1976).

The third area of criticism draws on this to some extent, but, rather than focusing on the family as an organisation that seeks to control men, it explores the nature of family life in closer detail and examines the subjugation of women. Thus, for a more insightful analysis into the *internal world* of the family, we now turn to feminist sociology.

Gendered division of labour

Feminism has its own history. The early feminist Mary Wollstonecraft argued that any focus on the rights of 'man' had to include the rights of women (Todd, 2000). Women also played key roles in the development of social work and welfare (see Chapter Two) and there was a rise of feminist thought towards the end of the late 19th century – often called 'first-wave' feminism. More recent feminist scholarship has exposed the extent to which women's contributions to society have been overlooked (Rowbotham, 1973). There are several strands to feminist sociology, yet they all contain core elements. The differences are largely ones of emphasis. For example, socialist feminists (Rowbotham et al, 1979) develop their position from a critical appraisal of capitalism; radical feminists focus on explicit gender differences and patriarchy (Millet, 1970; Rich, 1984; French, 1985); liberal feminists argue for equality within capitalism (Friedan, 1981); and black feminists point to how much of traditional 'white' feminist thought tends to ignore specific questions of 'race' (Carby, 1982; hooks, 1989; Mama, 1989). Feminism has enhanced scholarship by its desire to examine the personal sphere of women's lives. It did this by developing approaches that broke with more conventional modes of inquiry (hooks, 1989). Oakley, in her more recent work, has begun to revise some of this thinking, arguing for a combination of both qualitative and quantitative evidence, since she argues that it is only by establishing how widespread something is that a truly effective change strategy can be mounted (Oakley, 2005). Feminist enquiry has been vital in exploring the 'hidden' world of the family and we will now examine aspects of feminism as they relate to 'reproduction'.

Feminist analysis is helpful in exposing the way in which capitalism rests on a particular division of labour between men and women. Women are located very firmly in the home and not within the public arena of paid work. When women engage in paid work, it is lower paid and often part time (Grant et al, 2005). Wilson (1977) notes how women have traditionally been seen as a reserve army of labour, called into the workforce when needed, and then dispensed with. A frequently cited example of this is the role women played during the Second World War. When their labour was needed, childcare facilities were made readily available. After the war, these facilities were closed down, since the situation could go 'back to normal' – a slogan of the immediate postwar era. Esping-Andersen (1999), a political economist, develops a slightly different view, arguing that postwar prosperity meant that the option (he uses the word 'luxury') not to work was made available to all women, whereas previously it was largely restricted to middle-class women. Working-class women had always engaged in paid work, either in factories or as 'home workers'. Wilson (1977) suggests that the postwar shift was mainly from full-time to part-time workers. This was reflected in the dual rate of National Insurance contributions, which allowed married women to opt for a lower rate, with the consequence that they remained dependent on their husbands for benefits, including pension rights. Thus, the relationship between women and paid work resulted in a financial dependency on men through marriage. Feminist analyses of the 1970s onwards developed out of the division of labour *and* dependency on men.

Oakley (1985) examined the division of labour within the home and found that women were primary carers and homemakers. Indeed, over 20 years later, Bagilhole's (1997) research among women employed full time suggested that little had changed, despite legislation and a so-called 'more enlightened' attitude. Men tended to engage more with 'male' areas within the home – for example,

DIY, car maintenance – while women undertook tasks such as cleaning, washing and ironing. The roles adopted in the home substantiate the feminist claim that women service the male workforce, and in this way they 'reproduce' a set of necessary social relationships.

Women's roles, traditionally those of caring and nurturing, are reinforced through dominant images of what women should be like, especially in relation to the home. Leonard and Speakman (1986) point to the image of a woman as an 'angel in the home', with men being seen as providers and 'sturdy oaks'. In these analyses, caring has distinctly feminine qualities, further reinforcing the view that this is a 'natural' role for women (Twigg, 2000). Walby (1990) argues that this is far from natural but is rather a manifestation of the power of patriarchy to subjugate women. Thus, the benefit of a feminist analysis is that it focuses expressly on these 'taken-for-granted' gender relations and demonstrates that they are mainly a result of a social construction of specific gender roles. Thus feminism was connected to a movement that sought to end gender inequality and women's dependence on men.

The rise of the feminist movement in the 1970s coincided with significant changes, both in family composition and labour market participation. In the UK, changes to the divorce laws and the availability of the contraceptive pill combined to give greater degrees of freedom and control to a generation of women. The feminist slogan of the 1970s, 'the personal is political', arguably brought about changes in society and its organisation. The number of lone parents has risen consistently since the 1970s, divorce rates have increased and the number of cohabiting couples has risen steadily (Allan and Crowe, 2001). The reality of family life in the early 21st century is far removed from that analysed by Marx and Engels in the late 19th or even that investigated by 1970s' feminists. It is worth asking, however, to what extent the lives of women have actually changed. While the outward form of families has changed, has the experience of women shifted from one of dependence to 'independence'?

The sociology here is somewhat equivocal. While the demographics suggest substantial changes, the reality of women's lives still suggests levels of inequality and dependence – if not on 'men', then on the state. There has been a considerable body of research that points to the feminisation of poverty (Pearce, 1990; Daly and Rake, 2003; Lister, 2004) and the evidence reveals that high levels of poverty exist among lone parents (Gregg at al, 1999). The so-called breakdown of the family has led to claims that it has increased childhood poverty and levels of poverty for women. Campbell (1984) argued that for some young women, lone motherhood was a direct response to low-waged jobs and a sense of alienation, which brought about a form of acceptance as a mother. Further research into female poverty within families suggests strongly that after separation the level of income available to the woman actually increases even though the total income decreases (Graham, 1993).

Inequalities at work: wage inequality and the segregated labour market

Women's participation in the labour market has shown a gradual increase since the 1970s. There has been an increase in the rate of full-time as well as part-time employment. The increase in labour market participation is a feature shared by most European Union member states, and reflects increasing independence. This has been assisted by legislation and directives to 'ensure' equal pay for women, although the evidence suggests strongly that this is something that in many sectors women do not enjoy (Littlewood, 2004).

Even where women have attained equal pay with men, their lifetime earnings are likely to be less than men's. There could be two reasons for this. First, women often work in more casualised labour settings, with less of a career structure: simply put, women have jobs, rather than careers. Yet by far the most likely explanation for this is that it is women who take time out of work not just to give birth to children, but also to care for them. Davis and Ellis (1995) argue that this is 'enforced altruism'. Women may be entering into the world of informal care though choice, but, in truth, such choices are severely constrained. Thus, it could be argued that 'enforced altruism' has wider consequences. It not only affects lifetime earnings, but also has a significant impact on women's pensions: if their time in paid employment is less and their career prospects are damaged, the likelihood is that they will receive a lower pension. A real consequence, then, of being engaged in informal caring is that women are more likely to experience relative poverty in older age (Ginn et al, 2001; Scharf et al, 2002).

Even in a society that has a long tradition of supporting women in work and equality of labour rights, evidence suggests that it is still women who undertake the greater amount of informal care in the family. This is so in Sweden, where gender equality has been a clear policy aim since the 1930s and by many other countries' standards represents something of a high point in women's achievements. Studies of Sweden, however, by feminist writers in their research of informal care, have shown how it is women (not men) who usually undertake this work, and that, although Sweden may be more 'woman-friendly' than other European States, the myth of equality hides deep-rooted inequalities (Lewis and Åström, 1992; Jenson and Mahon, 1993). So, any changes to Sweden's welfare system are likely to have a disproportionate impact on women.

A further factor in relation to women, labour markets and reproduction is the nature of work women undertake. Looking at women's labour market participation more closely, it is clear that the labour market is segregated. This means that women are more likely to undertake certain jobs and the evidence suggests that women are over-represented in forms of employment that are related to 'care'. At the professional end of the labour market, women are employed in teaching (especially of younger children), nursing and social work, all areas with a strong 'caring' element. At the lower end of the scale, it is predominantly women who

St. Giles.
high women populated.

provide low-waged 'care' as classroom assistants, nurse auxiliaries, home helps and other social care workers as well as being frequently employed in the service sector in restaurants and hotels (Esping-Andersen, 1999).

There is one final element to be noted in relation to gendered labour. The emphasis on women being engaged in care work leaves them highly dependent for employment on the provision of welfare. Esping-Andersen (1999, 2002) sees this as a 'trade-off' – the one brings the other. The changing nature of work also has a class element, in that it has led to the creation of many low-paid jobs in the social care sector for women who essentially service the needs of other, more highly paid, women. Class therefore cannot be so readily divorced from gender in relation to aspects of 'reproduction' (Anderson, 2000; Littlewood, 2004).

So, the family serves as a site of 'reproduction', and the gendered nature of work, both within the home and in the public sphere, reinforces a series of views about women's roles and women's work. Finally, this chapter explores how the way ideas are presented helps sustain them.

Discourse as reproduction

Activity

Here is something that you can do over a couple of weeks. Collect items from different forms of media that relate to an aspect of reproduction or production and think carefully about how the issue is portrayed. Whenever you read this book, there will almost certainly be a current news item that relates to an aspect of either production or reproduction. Topics that tend to arise with alarming regularity are the family, which could include aspects of sexuality; youth crime and the 'breakdown of the family'; and migrant workers or minority ethnic groups. Consider how certain images and stereotypes are sustained or even challenged through the reporting.

When you have completed this exercise, it is probable that you will have seen that certain images and concepts are constantly used to sustain a particular view of a group of people or of an idea. These ideas help to shape a common-sense view of the world and are sometimes referred to as dominant ideology or discourses. A concept that is very much connected with the dominance of ideas is that of hegemony, a term developed by Gramsci. He was concerned with how ruling groups exercise leadership through the control and regulation of ideas, and how these ideas are disseminated. He argues that:

> [The dual perspectives of modern society] … are the levels of force and of consent, of authority and of hegemony … of the individual moment and of the universal moment, of agitation and of propaganda … reality is a product of the application of human will to the society of things. Only the man [*sic*] who wills something strongly can identify

the elements which are necessary to the realisation of his [*sic*] will. Hence to believe that one particular conception of the world and of life in general, in itself possesses a superior ... capacity is a crudely fatuous and superficial error. (Gramsci, 2003, pp 171-2)

This is a complex passage, but it sets out aspects of the duality or dialectic of modern society and invites us to consider the nature of the forces in contemporary society that are designed to bring about consent, to establish authority and to direct our thinking, for these are the 'realities' of which Gramsci is warning. Stuart Hall (1988) develops these concepts, both in relation to the family and society. He suggests that there is a duality at work and he calls this 'real consciousness'. As far as the family is concerned, the suggestion is that to dismiss this, as many Marxists do, simply as false is to disregard the reality of life. Indeed, others have commented that the family itself occupies a 'dual' space, for while it does reproduce the conditions for capital, it can also act as a possible site of resistance. Carby (1982) argues that for many black people, the family offers a haven of resistance to racism in the public world. Hall, however, goes on to say that despite this there is a dominance of ideas that comes from how certain events are presented. He calls this the distribution of knowledge:

> ... the social distribution of knowledge is skewed.... Ruling or dominant concepts of the world do not directly prescribe the mental content of the illusions that supposedly fill the heads of the dominated classes. But the circle of dominant ideas does accumulate the symbolic power to map or classify the world for others ... [this] becomes the horizon of the taken for granted. (Hall, 1988, p 44)

According to Hall, dominant ideas work by setting the parameters of what is common sense, and also by limiting the bounds of what can be conceptualised. Neither is it simply a case of these ideas being handed down from above. Hall and the German sociologist Habermas (1987, 1998) follow the idea of the dialectic, arguing that ideas are created by a form of dialogue and are not static, but rather are in a constant state of being negotiated and renegotiated. In this way, what is 'dominant' at one time can become effectively redundant at a future time, and there will be times when the conflict of ideas is plain to see. It could be argued, then, that what is being contested is the nature of society; it is not ideas for the sake of ideas in a Hegelian sense, but rather how ideas support economic interests that help to shape society and how we think about matters. Simply put, discourse, then, refers to how certain social phenomena are presented, and discussed, which in turn sets out how they become understood. An example here would be asylum seekers. There are sets of words and images, dominant in all forms of media representation, that are closely associated with people seeking asylum – 'bogus' and 'genuine' being obvious examples. These help construct a particular mental image of asylum seekers. The activity set earlier could provide other sets of examples.

The danger with focusing on discourse is that the analysis can all too often be of the language, rather than the real lives, of people it seeks to represent. That is not to suggest that discourses are not 'real', for the way language is used to create and maintain certain images is in itself a 'reality', but that for the people who experience a particular set of circumstances, daily life has a much more pressing urgency. This is evident when discussing families and the position of women. Feminist analysis has given considerable attention to the use of language (Spender, 1980; Gilligan, 1982; hooks, 1989) and how it sustains images of femininity that maintain women's subordinate position. Even at a seemingly trivial level, a male partner's willingness to 'help with the housework' cements the idea that this is really women's work, and thereby maintains a set of ideas about gender relations and the division of domestic labour.

At a wider level, discourse serves to establish as 'normal' ideas about work and society. Alternatives become 'unthinkable' and as such disappear or are marginalised. When it serves the interests of capital to have a shift in ideas, the discourse begins to change. As indicated earlier, when women were needed as workers during wartime, the discourse was concerned with promoting this and was backed up by policy changes. At the end of the war, the needs changed, and so did the discourse. Towards the end of the 20th century, there was a need for women's increased labour market participation in the UK. The discourse changed to encourage this, alongside shifts in policy to encourage (some would say coerce) lone mothers into paid work. This unfortunately did not sit easily with the other great discourse of the day, that of 'choice', and so another set of dualities began.

It has been suggested that British sociology has become too concerned with discourse analysis at the expense of actual 'scientific' examination of society (Stedman Jones, 2001). Discourse attains an importance not in itself, but rather for what it reveals about the nature of society. It is an entry point to exploring the nature of an exploitative and class-based society (Fairclough, 1995). The development of analysis drawn from Foucault (1994) began with an analysis of power and capital before moving away from this, seeing discourse as an aspect of power in its own right. The difficulty is that, as Stedman Jones (2001, p 222) argues, it is not words that actually *create* the social conditions people live in.

Reproduction: some concluding thoughts

Some of the ideas contained in this chapter are not easy to get to grips with. This is perfectly understandable and the reason is contained within the subject area itself. First, it concerns a combination of structures and discourses that seek to maintain dominant images and vested interests, and to set these out as being 'normal'. Thus, we are all subject to these 'images of normality' (Foucault, 1977, 1984). Therefore, stepping outside of them is difficult, and, to draw from Gramsci

(2003), it needs to be a specific act of will to enter into the dialectical process this entails.

Second, the whole area touches aspects of people's more intimate lives. The 1970s' feminists understood this all too well with their juxtaposition of the personal and political, for the sociology of reproduction more than anything else brings some of these conflicts and tensions directly into our private lives. Feminists developed an analysis of male power in society leading to the subjugation of women, but, of course, many of these writers also had relationships with men. This is not to undermine the analysis, but to demonstrate an underlying duality. Likewise, academics can cling to a Marxist analysis, yet at the same time benefit economically from society. Thus, the arena of reproduction heightens these tensions, bringing them into a sharper and often uncomfortable focus.

Third, finding a language to explain all of this has not proved to be an easy task and many writers have developed a range of concepts that, rather than making things clearer, have served to make things more difficult. The writers mentioned here – Foucault, Habermas and Gramsci, for example – are not easy to read and yet their works contain some important concepts that need to be understood to gain a clearer sense of the role of reproduction in contemporary society. The following chapter will seek to clarify this further by exploring how they can be applied to social work.

SIX

Social work and reproduction: regulation and family life

This chapter considers social work's response to theories of 'reproduction' and 'relationships', especially given the feminised nature of social work. It explores typical case scenarios and examines the extent to which social work practice supports traditional family responsibilities that underpin the post-industrial economy.

One of the aims is to demonstrate the significance of sociological approaches for practice, especially in relation to social exclusion and poverty, and to use different methods in doing so. Chapter Two, with its historical emphasis, identified some enduring tensions in social work that, it is suggested, are highlighted by a sociological approach, which necessitates an analysis of the relationship between people, society and social work. This was followed by an examination of the concept of 'production and work' and its relevance to social work practice. This chapter begins with some case studies and invites the reader to engage with a series of questions, drawn from the material relating to 'reproduction'. There follows a discussion of the case studies around those themes, incorporating further aspects of sociological inquiry.

When reading through the case studies, note down the links to the theories outlined in the previous chapter, and try to link these to theories of production identified in the earlier section, since the two are not easily separated. As you will no doubt soon become aware, there are many issues and discussion points in the case studies. This shows the interdisciplinary nature of social work. For example, in case study 1, you could think about the question of mother/parent–child attachment (Bowlby, 1953; Rutter, 1972; Howe, 1987; Fahlberg, 1994). You may also consider specific policy directives or legislative frameworks – the 1989 and 2004 Children Acts for the case studies relating to children, and the 1990 NHS and Community Care Act, 1995 Carers Act and 1995 Disability Discrimination Act for the case study relating to older people and disability. While these are important for social workers, it is likely to be the case that not only will they appear in other areas of your social work education and/or training, but they will also seem to dominate the way you are invited to think about certain questions. As stated in the introduction, sociology has an important part to play in the social work task. While acknowledging the contribution of other paradigms, you are encouraged to develop a sociological mindset for your practice and to deal only with the sociological concepts that you can identify in these scenarios.

It is suggested that you consider the following:

- What aspects of family life can you identify here that are subject to intervention?
- How do the case studies highlight the gendered division of labour either in the work place or the home?
- How do they connect to changing patterns of employment?
- What aspects of hegemonic discourse do they utilise?

The task need not be daunting, as some of these themes will be discussed later in the chapter. Chapter Two identified some enduring tensions in social work. You are encouraged to think about how these are present in the case studies and how you would deal with them in your own practice. The names have been changed and no mention is made of location, to ensure anonymity.

Case study 1

"I work with young mothers and their children and we do a whole lot of health promotion, for example, stopping smoking classes. We have a session each week where we talk about bringing children up, diet, reaching milestones, keeping appointments with the health visitor and so on. We have been trying to involve fathers in caring for the kids but not a lot of success there, they'd rather be down the pub – oh, yes, and we also run some classes which give the parents job-seeking skills."

Social worker, employed by a Sure Start Project

Case study 2

"I've been working with some kids who don't go to school. Emma is a real handful and won't go. I've tried making appointments to see her in the mornings even, but her mother says she won't get up. We took her to school once but she just bunked off after registration. It's been like this for a number of years, and I've had to tell her mother that she could be prosecuted (yes, the mother not Emma) if she doesn't get there. There was a time when Emma was being assessed by an educational psychologist but her mother didn't keep the appointments, and then Emma was permanently excluded from school, so nothing came of it in the end. Some mothers have already been prosecuted and even sent to prison, but Emma doesn't seem to care what will happen. The policy is in place and I really think that is an option ... her mother is at her wits' end, but there really isn't much else we can do."

Education social worker in a multidisciplinary team

Case study 3

"I'm working with Gwen, who is in her eighties. She's quite a bright spark, but not good on her feet and recently she's had a lot of falls. It really reached the point where she needed support to stay in her own home. To start with, she wanted to go into a home, believe it or not, but when I explained we didn't do that unless there were really serious problems she seemed happy to stay. There wasn't a lot of funding available for the home care though, and certainly not enough to meet her needs. Anyway, I got in touch with her daughter, who lives about five miles away, and told her of the situation. She wasn't keen to help out, to be honest, because she works part time. Anyway, I managed to persuade her to support her mother and then organised the home care service around this. I don't think she was that pleased, but as I said to her, she is Gwen's daughter."

Social worker, adults' services team

These case studies throw up a number of areas of exploration, but the most important observation is that most of the interventions targeted women. Social work's concern with family, relationships within the family and even relationships between families and society are generally mediated through women as recipients of services and targets of intervention (Wilson, 1977; Ungerson, 1983, 1987; Twigg, 2000; Scourfield, 2003).

This links very clearly to the twin aspects of the reproduction of capitalism through the family and of gender relationships. The essential argument here is that by focusing on women's traditional gender roles, social work becomes complicit in 'reproducing' these conditions. Of course, it is not nearly as simple as that, since if we also look at the enduring tensions, you might have thought that all of these areas or possible interventions contained some aspects that were either necessary or even positive. This takes us to the heart of the book's unifying theme, that of the dialectical nature of social work. Put another way, it shows that social workers have to 'live out the contradictions'. There can be no doubt that this is not an easy position for social workers to be in, but it is the position many social workers actually occupy. This chapter examines how aspects of the sociological theory can be applied to the case studies, using them as a springboard to explore social work with different service user groups and to begin to show the dialectical position of social workers.

Social work and family support: regulating the family?

Whereas theories of production focus on the public world of work and paid employment, the theories of reproduction focus upon the private world of family life. The previous chapter introduced some sociological ideas about the place of the family in society, and developed into a discussion of feminist theories about the gendered division of labour and 'caring' work. This chapter aims to develop these ideas and to link them to the social work task of supporting families, especially families with young children. The very nature of this role takes us to the heart of at least one enduring dilemma, namely, that of 'care or control'. In fact, it is possible to question whether there can be care without some element of control. One of the difficulties for contemporary social workers is something that has already been hinted at in previous chapters: how much has the fundamental premise of society changed, and how great an impact does this have on sociological theories that seem to be located in a different era? To what extent do some of the feminist theories about discrimination, patriarchy and male domination still apply? Have ideas about women's position actually changed or have they become part of a backdrop of sociological insights that are then disregarded by social workers in practice?

Oakley (1987) argued that one of the achievements of feminism was that it showed the family to be a source of ambivalence for women. In her writings on gender and family life, Oakley frequently referred to women as being invisible. In relation to functionalism, she argues that women are 'over-visible' and that "a way of seeing is a way of not seeing", drawing a basic distinction between women as providers of emotional support and men as providers of financial support (Oakely, 2005, pp 204-5). Oakley also argues that it is important not only to expose the *experience* of women, something that clearly distinguishes a 'feminist' research methodology (Dominelli, 1997), but also to locate this within the broader picture:

> Women and other minority groups, above all, need 'quantitative' research, because without this, it is difficult to distinguish between personal experience and collective oppression. Only large-scale comparative data can determine to what extent the situations of men and women are structurally differentiated. (Oakley, 2005, p 249)

Were this to be applied to social work, it would suggest that social workers need to ensure that they have an awareness of the large-scale trends, as well as the experiences they encounter. Indeed, in the authors' experience, social workers do come across situations that are similar often enough for them to provide more than just 'personal experience' but also to suggest structural trends to be explored. But, and this is an important 'but', social workers deal with experiences on a day-to-day basis and these are all too often encountered in terms of individual pathologies. Thus, women, as the main targets of intervention become 'blamed' as the cause of the 'problem'. Scourfield (2003) provides examples of this in his interviews with social workers. The structural causes of people's difficulties were well known, but the focus of practice was with individuals, and created the impression that they were to 'blame'. Milner (1993) demonstrated quite clearly how men often 'disappeared' from social work practice, and Wise (1995) questions the nature of the social work relationship, especially in relation to women who abuse their children. What they all have in common is that, despite the different positions they reflect in relation to the *nature* of family support, the target of that support is *women*. Milner argues that the very use of the term 'family' by social workers is often little more that a synonym for women.

When considering aspects of childcare, it is women who form the target group for social work intervention. The nature of case study 1 should also provide sufficient evidence about the extent of the regulatory aspects at work here (diet, child development and stopping smoking all being important aspects), yet how many of those same 'problems' are connected with the poverty of the women's environments and living situations? In their 1989 study, Walkerdine and Lucey argue that often what is seen as 'good child rearing' reflects the dominance of middle-class views on the matter. Working-class women have lives beset by different stresses and pressures and develop different child-rearing practices. Crucially, though, Walkerdine and Lucey argue that these are *different*, not inferior, and may even be more beneficial. The concerns of social workers over the past 150 years return here: are the 'victims' of poverty being blamed?

A sociological analysis would suggest that this is more than a possibility. The contradiction for social workers is that to do nothing to attempt to make a difference in people's lives in the here and now is to leave those difficult relationships and personal situations untouched. The circumstances could therefore potentially worsen and result in even more 'controlling' interventions, for example, the removal of children. The contradictions of the social work role are therefore clear and the enduring tension for social work evident: 'care' is often another way of exerting 'control'.

Social work and education: regulating young people?

The link between social work and education is one that can be traced back to the earliest days of modern social work. The work of Mary Carpenter, discussed in Chapter Two, is an example of this. In many European countries, there is a specific branch of social work called 'social pedagogy'. This is based on many of the principles of educational development, even though in more recent times it has become almost synonymous with more mainstream social work activity (Wieler, 2000). Despite this, there is relatively little research that focuses expressly on social work and education, although the work of Blyth and Milner (1997) is a notable exception. The educational system itself has also long been associated with the regulation of young people, especially in relation to their future place in the labour market (Willis, 1978). The argument here is that education is a central feature in the reproduction of capitalism and contemporary society. Of course, this does not mean that formal education is only related to functionalist ideas. Indeed, education is very often a means by which people's horizons are broadened and a range of opportunities opened up for them. In the UK, the development of universal secondary education in 1948 opened up a range of possibilities for working-class children, as did aspects of the comprehensive system in the 1960s and, more recently, the 'widening participation' agenda in higher education. These are significant UK policy developments, but they have also been mirrored elsewhere.

There can be little doubt that without suitable educational attainment, the life chances of many children and young people are considerably reduced, therefore any attempt to maximise this will have beneficial consequences for the young people concerned. There is also clear evidence that poor educational attainment is directly linked to poverty, inequality and social exclusion. Educational attainment is rightly seen as a possible way of reducing poverty (Esping-Andersen, 2002; SEU, 2004) and its importance for those groups who experience other forms of exclusion should also be acknowledged. Data for 2003 place black and Pakistani/Bangladeshi boys at the wrong end of the table of educational attainment in the UK (ONS, 2005). When this is set against the class position of those young people, the correlation between low educational attainment and all forms of exclusions becomes even clearer, with Pakistani and Bangladeshi people in the UK experiencing considerable levels of poverty (Palmer et al, 2005). Muslim children do less well, not because of an adherence to Islam, but because of their position in UK society. This is the subject of considerable debate within the Muslim community in many UK cities. The leader of Birmingham Central Mosque has reportedly blamed the lack of opportunities and educational attainment for Muslims on 'Islamophobia', whereas in the same report a female Muslim local councillor argued that this was a problem of resource allocation and not a 'faith' issue (Richards, 2006). Educational attainment is also discussed in Chapter Ten, and this illustrates how many sociological concepts intersect and can be applied to the same areas in different ways. One of the key failings of social work over the years has been the very poor attainment of children and young people who were 'looked after' by the local authority and which is being belatedly addressed by the *Every Child Matters* initiative (HM Government, 2004). So, why should this type of work cause difficulties for social workers?

First, the context of this type of work seems to be located primarily in enforcing attendance. This is part of a policy agenda that has been described as 'tough love' (Stepney et al, 1999; Jordan with Jordan, 2000). The measures are essentially coercive and ultimately seek to 'punish' the parent who fails to send their child to school. Case study 2 identifies this quite clearly: while a measure of support can be put into place, the ultimate sanction is one of punishment. Given that there have been parents – usually lone mothers – imprisoned by the courts for their children's school non-attendance, this is not just some theoretical position being advanced, but one that has real consequences for parents.

Second, there is little evidence that attainment is increasing and therefore aspects of the relationship between education and poverty seem likely to remain. The focus on the children of 'poor parents' who live in socially deprived neighbourhoods deflects from the realities of those very areas. The suggestion that the way to improve education is by extending the principle of 'choice' reinforces the limited choices open to many people. A relatively straightforward piece of local investigation will illustrate this. In estate agents' advertisements for houses in any local area, there will doubtless be some properties described as being in the 'catchment area' of, or near to, a good local school. A quick look at what type of houses these are, or, more tellingly, what prices they are asking compared with similar houses outside the school's area, will reveal them to be more expensive. This means that poorer people will not be able to move to that area, thereby preserving its relatively 'privileged' status. This will also have a direct relationship to black and minority ethnic groups, who, as we have already seen, are more likely to be poor, and their children, especially boys, experience further disadvantages within the educational system itself (Hunte, 2004). In turn, this means that those who are poor are more likely to be locked into living in areas with schools with fewer resources. Thus, there is a clear relationship between poverty and education that cannot be broken by merely enforcing attendance (McKnight et al, 2005; Evans, 2006).

Third, there is the question of the curriculum. There are strong arguments to suggest that certain subjects (history, for example) are presented in a certain way, promoting a certain interpretation, usually a 'top-down' version of events (Marwick, 1970; Stedman-Jones, 1984). It is not the intention to explore this here, but it should be noted that some schools in certain locations are more likely to offer 'vocational' programmes for GCSE than academic ones. This is not to say that vocational courses are of little use, or that only academic achievements are valued, but it does mean that if a young person attends a school with an emphasis on vocational subjects, their opportunity, even the expectation, of entering higher education is lowered. Willis's (1978) findings seem to have a strong contemporary application. The education *system* still largely determines people's life chances.

There is a tension for social workers in these considerations, which a sociological analysis brings to the fore. By focusing upon an agenda of school attendance, social workers and others are engaged in measures to reduce social exclusion and poverty. Yet, such a functionalist approach to education masks underlying inequalities within the education system itself. Social work's enduring dilemmas of care or control, punishment or treatment, are clearly present. This also raises questions about the need to become involved in a political agenda, for if there is a link between poor schools and deprivation, this has to be addressed in a campaigning manner. If not, social work reverts to providing individual solutions to structural deficiencies.

Social work and older people: regulating care?

Social work with older people is an area where the dialectical tensions of 'reproduction' are clear. Moves towards increased levels of domiciliary support have been very well documented, although, as Lewis and Glennerster (1996) demonstrated shortly after the implementation of the 1990 NHS and Community Care Act in 1993, the greatest challenge still facing local authorities is the tension between 'needs' and available resources. It is interesting to note that, in the UK, the legislation that gave this its final impetus was the 1990 NHS and Community Care Act. This legislation was arguably the culmination of a series of economically and politically motivated changes to the relationship between central and local government, and it sprang from the neoliberal economic agenda of the Thatcher government. While there have been several attempts to argue that good domiciliary care is not cheap (Lewis and Glennerster, 1996), the reality remains that funding for this area, though growing, is much less than it would have been if other forms of residential and sheltered housing care had been developed. The economic reality of domiciliary care is that there does not need to be as much capital investment in buildings: the older person stays in their own home for as long as possible. This has shifted the nature of intergenerational dependence and a critical feature is the prerequisite for both economic security and social inclusion, which is at odds with current economic policies, which seek to minimise the economic costs of ageing (Walker, A., 2006). So, by promoting aspects of independence and community-based care, social work manages to combine the needs of older people with economic principles.

Williams (2001) confirms this, arguing that the state wants simultaneously to reduce the costs of caring that it bears and to attempt to regulate care so that it is delivered both safely and effectively. Harris (2002) locates care in a citizenship context, arguing that policy seeks to incorporate caring as an expression of good citizenship and social obligations. We cannot provide a complete overview of the concept of care, but it is important to note that Graham (1983, p 13) makes a case to distinguish between what caring means for people and what it entails. The action of caring, therefore, has meaning to both the caregiver and the person receiving the care. Ungerson (1983, 1987) also identifies aspects of social taboos that may place limits on who does what in relation to caring for either older people or children, and the gender stereotype of women as natural carers is a crucial factor in these developing social relations (Twigg, 2000; Carabine, 2004).

Older people as recipients of care are not the whole picture. Arber and Ginn (1990) demonstrate that around 40% of older people are caregivers, usually for their partner. In a similar vein, Ackers and Dwyer (2002) show that there are considerable intergenerational aspects of caring activity across the European Union. An important point here is that many older people look after grandchildren in an 'informal', that is, unpaid, capacity to allow their own grown-up children to maximise their earning potential by not paying childcare costs.

As case study 3 encapsulates, however, there are various tensions for social workers in ensuring the care of older people. First, encouraging an older person to remain in their own home can be seen as social work promoting both independence and freedom of choice. It should be noted, however, that if the older person 'chooses' not to stay in their own home, it is likely that, in the words of a social worker of some years' experience, "they will be encouraged to think again, and we'd focus on all the things they would be 'losing'".

Choice, therefore, is only promoted if it is the 'right' choice. The case study shows how the social worker actually encouraged the older person to remain at home. For many older people, their choice is to stay in their home, and when this occurs it is easier for the social worker to support this.

The case study then focuses on the essentials of the support: how much is it going to cost and who is going to provide it? In a climate of economic restraint, funding becomes a central issue and it is here that 'citizenship' or even filial duty becomes important. The crucial factor is the mother–daughter relationship and the ties of 'duty' that can be used to encourage unpaid, informal care. The social worker then builds the paid care around what the daughter can provide. Material in the previous chapter relating to gendered divisions of labour should be readily applicable here, since the example shows how the assumption that women are the carers still dominates the agenda. In the case study, the social worker uses the blood tie to construct the relationship of care around duty and responsibility: the daughter's paid work is seen as being of lesser importance. Had we continued with the case study, we would also have seen how the paid care workers were also women and low-paid workers. Thus, in the provision of care, social workers inadvertently draw on the position of women as carers, and on the new army of low-paid care workers (Littlewood, 2004). Kofman and Sales (1998) identify the relatively low status of female migrants in the European labour market, and their over-representation in the care sector. Anderson (2000) makes the point that often the need for an army of paid care workers, even if this frequently means working women employing home-based help, is mainly a question of lifestyle, and this reinforces aspects of capitalist production and class-based gender inequality. Care therefore underpins an intersection between gender and class, and interestingly, given that women form the greater part of the social work workforce, it is women who regulate this.

Social work and families: maintaining the discourse?

The final area examined in this chapter in relation to social work practice in general and the case studies in particular is that of discourse. A theme that can be traced throughout is that of the family, and this will be used to demonstrate how social work underpins this aspect of contemporary discourse.

As already discussed, much of sociological theory, especially in recent years, has been concerned with discourse. Foucault (1984) was particularly concerned with sexuality and this has been incorporated into aspects of social work literature, even though at times it has been controversial, for example, in relation to same-sex adoption. Many of the standard generic social work texts deal with discourse and how it can shape the way people see others, especially in relation to race and gender (Dominelli, 1997; Thompson, 1997). More specifically, Cheetham (1972) and Owusu-Bempah and Howitt (2000) have written about how discourse generates certain social constructions in relation to race. Gender is also well covered in the social work literature (Dominelli, 1997), and Scourfield (2003) provides a discussion of discourse around masculinity, as does Pringle (1995). More recently, the rise of disability rights has also had a substantial impact on social work, showing how discourses of disability help maintain disabled people in dependent positions (Oliver, 1990; Shakespeare, 1993; Barnes et al, 1999). The focus on care has led to the identification of 'discourses of care', which sees caregiving, especially when the caregiver is female, as 'natural' (Daly, 2002; Mooney, 2004). J. Lewis (2000) demonstrates how this is the case using a cross-national comparison. Much of the focus on care is also a focus on the family. Whereas 'family' was once a highly contested term, often indicating oppression (Segal, 1983), the term has now become one that is inclusive of all types of form and arrangement (Lentell, 1998). This could be construed as evidence of a renewed family-based discourse promoted by social work.

The concept of the family in social work has been subject to much less critical analysis in more recent years. Feminists developed a critique of the family and there is an extensive analysis of how there is a clearly defined discourse about the family that supports a traditional, nuclear and patriarchal family (Segal, 1983; Leonard and Speakman, 1986). As demonstrated earlier, the nature of the contemporary family has, however, changed quite markedly over the years, with a considerable rise in lone-parent families since the 1970s.

Meanwhile, feminists and other 'radical' groups within social work once held a largely critical view of the family, identifying it as a dangerous place for women and children (MacLeod and Saraga, 1988). While it is still the case that the term 'family intervention' is used mainly for women (Milner, 1993), the analysis on the potentially negative impact of the family has largely disappeared.

As the case studies show, the language of current social work policy utilises the family in service delivery. There is a generally held view, for example, that children are 'better off in their own families' and this has led to a whole raft of services that arguably place the needs of adult family members above those of their children and represent a move away from children's rights (Franklin, 1995, 2002). Scourfield (2003), who is largely 'pro-family', counters this by suggesting that the discourse around the family could support the removal of children of families perceived to be failing, although he would acknowledge that this is usually after considerable efforts to maintain children in their birth family.

Moves towards gay and lesbian fostering and adoption, although themselves subject to criticism, largely stand in this 'pro-family trend'. The UN Convention on Children's Rights identifies the 'right to family life' and this has become extensively promoted throughout the UK since 2000 (Franklin, 2002). Changes in adoption legislation have been linked to this and the family is promoted as the counter-discourse to residential care. The economic implications of this should not be lightly dismissed: the family is cheaper.

Other trends are being encouraged by social work; for example, the identification and extension of 'kinship care' or networks, and the 'family group conference'. This development, introduced from New Zealand (Nixon et al, 2005), seeks to identify aspects of the extended family and use them as part of either a network of care, or as caregivers. While this may have positive results for children in some situations, it is premised on a positive view of the family, thereby promoting a particular view of family discourse. The use of grandparents as carers should also be viewed in relation to the Ackers and Dwyer (2002) research in the previous section.

Social work monitors the patterns of family life, for example, child rearing and interaction, and there is unquestionably an argument to suggest that this is something that is based on middle-class mothers' values, who usually have different lifestyles to working-class mothers (Walkerdine and Lucey, 1989). While there is a lengthy history of this type of intervention and surveillance – often with positive results, it should be said (De Groot, 1996) – there is a continuation of the tensions that beset the Victorian social workers. Despite its rhetoric of 'empowerment', social work remains an activity that is concerned with surveillance, and, more importantly, this surveillance often renders structural deficits as personal problems.

Part Four
Consumption

SEVEN

New forms of relations and inequality?

While production and reproduction have a long sociological history, it is only more recently that consumption has attained greater sociological attention. This chapter examines consumption, arguing that it has a contradictory force of its own. It brings about new forms of inequality and exclusion for the poor, but it can also be a means of inclusion, for example, the 'pink pound' (the combined spending power of gay people). Understanding the nature of consumption and its broader linkages to production is crucial for social workers' understanding of their service users' social position.

Consumption and contemporary society

Activity

What do you think of when you hear the word 'consumption' in relation to contemporary society? How much of a consumer are you?

> History is from day to day, and nothing … has been more daily than keeping shop or going shopping. (Adburgham, 1989, p viii)

Miles (2001)[1] offers a comprehensive discussion about consumption, including summaries of the work of leading theorists, and how this relates to 'the real world'. He argues that one of the difficulties with the term is that it is so much a part of our lives, we do not even think about it, we just do it – even those who have relatively little money. Miles engages in a sociological discussion about the distinction between 'consumption' and 'consumerism'. This book is more concerned with the processes of consumption as they relate to capitalism and production.

Production refers to what is produced or manufactured; broadly speaking, it refers to work, that is, how we earn money. Consumption in its broadest sense refers to what we 'consume', that is, what we spend. This chapter began by saying that consumption is a new concept, but it is important to emphasise that what is new is the *sociological study* of consumption, which has developed considerably in recent years. Marx, in his analysis of capitalism, was quite clear that markets had to be generated for the goods that were produced and that consumption could not be easily separated from production. Gough (1978) cites from Marx's *Grundrisse*:

> Production thus produces consumption; first, by furnishing the latter with material; second, by determining the manner of consumption; third, by creating in consumers a want for its products as objects of consumption. It thus produces the object, the manner and the desire for consumption. (Marx, 1968, in Gough, 1978, p 222)

This identifies two important points. First, there is a distinction to be made between consumption as a concept and the consumer. Second, markets will create within consumers the desire for a product, a 'want', as opposed to a 'need', which is seen as universal (Doyal and Gough, 1991). Marx placed an emphasis on what was 'consumed'. The idea that an object can have a value greater than its 'use' value emanates from Marx's general analysis of labour and relates strongly to the concept of alienation as discussed in Chapter Three, in that the producer often does not enjoy the product of his labour. So, the economic system is an important feature in our lives, not just because of what we produce, but also because of what we consume.

We live in a globalised economy (Yeates, 2001) and as a result it is often held that contemporary society has changed from the one Marx observed. One feature of the dialectic, as noted earlier, is a difference between how things seem to be *different*, and the extent to which things have remained the *same*. In the West, many of the large-scale industries have closed down and have been relocated to other parts of the world. The increased prosperity in the West and changes in aspects of production have led to a changing relationship between what is 'made' and what is 'consumed'. Many of the cheap goods available on the UK high street are produced in parts of the world where production costs are exceptionally low. The exploitation of child labour is a factor in the low production costs, and hence the low prices. For example, an ILO report (ILO, The Director General, 2006) indicated that throughout the world around one in seven children between the ages of five and 17 are engaged in work on a daily basis, and that many of them receive very low wages. In the UK, the minimum wage does not apply to those under 21. The exploitation of workers elsewhere is often a hidden feature of Western consumption and, moreover, the developing world is dependent on patterns of consumption in the West (Latouche, 1993). This could be viewed as a shift in production, and UK consumers could be seen as 'affluent' in world terms. After all, we provide the market for cheap goods produced overseas and benefit from the exploitation of workers. So, in this sense, consumption is a new area of study, but an age-old phenomenon.

As Marx's work suggests, the activity of consumption extracts additional value from production. Zukin (1990, summarised in Miles, 2001) argued that whereas previously people gained some meaning from the work they did, patterns of late

20th-century consumption changed the nature of such meanings. What concerns us now, he suggests, is not so much the effort of making goods, but rather the buying of them. It is also a shift from a more public world of work to a personal world of style and consumer choice, fuelled by desires rather than necessity. It is this shift of 'meaning' that has attracted the attention of sociologists and there is a close relationship between consumption and culture (McCracken, 1990; Lee, 1993; McRobbie, 1994; Miles, 1998).

To take this a stage further, we have to think about how we are encouraged to consume. Advertisers focus on 'dreams': the 'dream holiday', the 'dream car' and the 'dream home' take consumption out of the public world and locate it right at the heart of the private and intimate world of relationships and desires. We do not have to buy the product to dream about it. Our shopping fantasies are sufficient to underscore Marx's early assertion that consumption is premised on 'wants' being transformed into 'needs' (Gough, 1978, p 222).

On the other hand, consuming is a major part of most people's lives. Consumption, and the goods available in a fully developed capitalist economy, create the image of bright lights. West Berlin was developed to reflect Western consumption, with its bright neon signs and shopping areas. This contrasted with the relative drabness of the East. The visitor to modern-day Berlin will still be struck with the differences between the old East and West. To put it another way, consumption is capitalism in full colour: production is, by contrast, monochrome. It is perfectly possible, when describing Western society, to say that we are all consumers and, moreover, that the strength of the economy and prospects for economic growth are heavily dependent on 'consumer confidence'. Keegan (2006) hints at the extent to which consumer spending is a critical factor in economic growth and a strong economy, when reporting on the belief in Germany that the 2006 World Cup would boost consumer confidence. Balakrishnan (2006) also noted that German consumers were spending more and that this would provide a welcome boost to the economy, especially in the retail sector. It is not the intention here to engage in economic analysis, but a simple review of the financial pages of daily newspapers reveals how important consumer spending is and how many column inches are devoted to it. So, how we spend our money is of prime *economic*, and not just *personal*, importance.

So, while consumption is full of personal meaning, it is actually a matter of public importance, for it is needed to sustain economic growth. This is a continuing feature of capitalism, as is the creation of a particular market for a given set of goods. Consumption, however, has developed in quite a different direction for most people than that of merely markets and commodities. The dominance of consumption and its attendant consumers in contemporary society is not only about economic performance, but also about how consumption has become inextricably linked with culture and identity and has succeeded in commodifying our private worlds (Zukin, 1990).

The shift from an economy based on production to one based on consumption is, for some writers, a sign of a postmodern society. The authors dispute this, suggesting that modernist approaches still have much to offer, but acknowledge that the *nature* of capitalism *is* changing, especially in the West. Ritzer and Goodman (2004) develop the argument that postmodern society is based on consumerism and *individual* patterns of consumption and that, crucially, the growth of consumption, particularly in the service sector, brings with it an inevitable decline in production. Production has, however, shifted its site, as capitalism seeks out both new markets and greater profit. Nevertheless, the more recent sociological writing about the nature of consumption still needs to be explored, for it is the case that within the UK consumption has acquired an importance it previously did not have. So, there has been a shift in the nature of capitalism, away from the importance of work, and towards the importance of consumption. There is a meaning, a purpose, attached to consumer goods or fashion, which has been the subject of more recent sociological investigation.

Campbell (1987, 1995) links this to the development of capitalism. In its early stages, there was a need for a strong work ethic and for money to be reinvested. This was supported by developments in Protestantism, based on 'self-denial' (Tawney, 1961; Weber, 1992). This coincided with the rise of the Romantic Movement in the arts and literature, as people began to place an emphasis on pleasure. Campbell makes a distinction between what is pleasure and what brings about satisfaction, and in a consumer society people seek pleasure through consumption. It is not the act of consumption that is important, but the meaning that is given to the goods that are bought.

Consumption as identity

Activity

Think about why you shop and consume. Is it a purely functional activity (we consume to survive) or does it carry elements of something more important to you? How far is your identity shaped and determined by how and what you consume?

The idea that consumption reveals to others aspects of our own identity is nothing new. Veblen, writing originally in 1899, in a work that has subsequently gained far greater importance, wrote about conspicuous consumption. He identified a 'leisure class' that was able to assert a particular social position by what it consumed. So, in relation to the actual goods, there were items that acquired a value far greater than any use value the goods might have (see Chapter Three). To give an example, a handbag has a particular set of uses and its use value reflects these. To a greater or lesser extent, the use value of similar handbags would be roughly equivalent. If, however, the handbag were made by a well-known luxury fashion house (for example, Gucci) the value of the handbag would be far greater than any use value it may have. The Gucci bag is not just any bag: it has a symbolic value that reflects the holder's social status and position in society. As Veblen (1994, p 46) argued, "the consumption of these excellent goods is an evidence of wealth". So, there is a social and cultural role to consumption and not just an economic one. Veblen studied the aspiring middle class at the turn of the 19th century. Consumption in the early 21st century embraces all classes and social groups.

Expressions of status and identity are closely related and with the expansion of cheaper clothing and consumer goods, working–class people could participate in what has become a huge market inviting mass participation. To do this, consumption has to be something more than just meeting a need. Bauman (1998) developed the argument that society engages its members through their consumption, whereas previously people were engaged through production. We can almost reduce this to a party conversation. Rather than beginning a conversation with the question 'What do you do for a living?', it is not uncommon for people to ask 'Where did you buy that shirt?'. Trends and fashions creating certain social 'norms' all combine to construct a reality that we, as consumers, literally 'buy into'. Miles identifies this in relation to 'youth lifestyles'. He argues that whether or not young people actually consume, they are all affected by consumption, which offers the flexible lifestyle choices young people desire (Miles, 2000, p 158). This is not just relevant to young people. Processes of consumption have affected everyone and are a significant development in society, suggesting the commodification of identity, something that can be bought, sold and, arguably, changed according to fashion. Put another way, when production dominated society, many people *were what they did*: a miner, a nurse, a doctor, a university lecturer. Now, people are what they *consume*.

Before discussing consumption and identity in more detail, let us return to the work of Campbell. Campbell sees consumption not so much as an act of buying products, but rather as a state of mind or acts of 'daydreaming' (1987, p 77). Veblen saw conspicuous consumption as being a practical manifestation of status and success; the Gucci bag or Armani suit tells everyone that you are a successful person. Campbell, by contrast, does not see consumption as being the sign of a satisfied society, but rather an act of *dissatisfaction*. Consumption becomes an activity based on people's illusions. They are not satisfied with their lot and seek any pleasures that consumption can offer. He argued that consumers are never fully satisfied and therefore will consume even more in a futile attempt to gain satisfaction. In other words, the greater the level of dissatisfaction, the greater the 'need' to seek fulfilment through consumption. Drawing on this idea, Lury (1996) suggested that social status *can* be attained through consumption, in ways that otherwise would be out of reach, in the fulfilment of dreams and desires. Miles (1998) identifies a paradox of consumption: the realities are hidden from the consumer precisely because they have the power to consume.

These ideas have entered into everyday language: so-called 'retail therapy' to get over an unhappy event is a manifestation of this. Buying new products, be they hi-fi equipment, cars, clothes or even holidays, fulfils a set of illusions we hold about what these products can bring for us. We do not buy a dream car; we actually buy our own dream of what the car can bring us. Think about how advertisers sell cars and holidays: the consumer is presented with a certain image. The Welsh tourist board, for example, does an excellent job of promoting Wales, but the brochures rarely indicate that Wales is one of the wettest places in the UK. In fact, the brochures are usually full of blue skies and smiling, dry people. Few people imagine a dream holiday to a place where it rains. In sport, the Champions League is advertised with the slogan 'Live the dream', yet for the majority of European football clubs the dream is unattainable. For some, the reality of chasing the dream has led to near bankruptcy, as in the case of Leeds United in 2004 (Britcher, 2004). It is not just the aspirations of football clubs that are built on borrowed money, but those of many people. As consumption becomes important, it is worth noting that for many people the pursuit of satisfaction through consumption has led to increased levels of debt (Haurant, 2006), and this is explored in Chapter Eight.

Contemporary capitalism and consumption is built on people chasing their dreams and translating these into consumer goods. When people are denied fulfilment through their work as a result of alienation, they will seek meaning elsewhere. The roots of dissatisfaction lie in the nature of society. One can almost see a new cycle of exploitation here: alienation brought about by the nature of work leads to dissatisfaction, but rather than this provoking a crisis within capitalism, it provokes disillusioned consumers who consume even more, thereby creating greater profits. Whereas religion might have been the 19th-century 'sigh of the oppressed creature' (Marx, 1844, cited in Jordan, 1972, p 74) it is possible that consumption has become its 21st-century replacement.

Before ending the exploration of the sociology of consumption and identity, we turn to the work of Pierre Bourdieu, who studied the French middle classes and their lifestyles. Bourdieu's work is more readily associated with the concept of social capital, which will be examined in Chapter Ten, but his ideas have relevance for understanding consumption. He argued that taste and patterns of consumption differ according to social group or social class. Consumption therefore tells people who you are, reflecting actual capital (as Veblen suggested) as well as social capital. Social boundaries are not merely created by patterns of consumption, but the same boundaries maintain and sustain such patterns. Whereas social class was once determined by production, in a society based on consumption, this is an indicator of class. Thus, people who try to enter a particular class can have their 'true' class revealed when faced with situations that are unknown to them and as such they are unfamiliar with the 'appropriate' behaviour. McDowell (1992) demonstrates this in relation to male dress codes, suggesting that "fear is one of the strongest motives for conformist dressing" (1992, p 98). Although he was writing about what is now a somewhat outmoded convention of wearing a tie to a 'good' restaurant, the sentiment remains. By not following the dress code, social position is possibly betrayed and McDowell suggests that traditional barriers between the classes were maintained in such ways.

Consumption, culture and gender

It is worth considering the extent to which consumption is structured along gender lines in a consumer society. Much of the literature associated with aspects of personal consumption focuses on women. For example, Adburgham's interesting account of how shopping changed the 19th century focuses on fashions for women – indeed the subtitle clarifies this, should there be any doubt: *Where, and in what manner the well-dressed Englishwoman bought her clothes.*

Feminist writers have long pointed out how images of femininity have been socially constructed and mediated through fashion (McRobbie, 1997). Miles (2001) focuses on consumption and men, an analysis taken up here, first, because it shifts the focus away from more traditional and even stereotyped female consumption, and, second, because it seems to be an area of a marketing shift, and one that demonstrates the need for capitalism to develop new markets. The other chosen example is football and rugby league because these large spectator sports are doubtless significant in the lives of many of the people who are service users.

The case of Leeds United Football Club, discussed earlier, opens up the area of the 'consumption of sport' (Miles, 1998). Clubs compete not just as teams on the playing field, but also as businesses in the corporate world, seeking to promote their 'brand'. It is not just football that has been subject to the business language of branding, as Denham (2000, 2004) argues in relation to rugby league. Denham attributes the rejuvenation of rugby league to the financial backing and marketing of Sky Television. Tellingly, he notes that the names given to clubs were designed to shift the public and marketing attention away from the game's traditional northern, working-class roots. For example, Warrington is now known as the Wolves, whereas its previous nickname, the Wires, reflected an aspect of local production.

When asked whether rugby league could ever be successful in the South, Ian Lenagan, the Chairman of Harlequins Rugby League Club, commented:

> Now we've got the famous Harlequins brand to slide over the top, we're marketing rugby league and the club professionally everywhere from South West Trains to pub toilets – ladies' and gents' – and taking advantage of the sea change in attitude between union and league ... and already season ticket sales, corporate hospitality sales and opening-match ticket sales are beyond budget. (Lenagan, 2006)

The key words – Harlequins brand, marketing rugby league, corporate hospitality – are the words of business and marketing rather than of sport, and certainly not of a sport originally connected with working-class life in northern England.

While sport has probably always been seen as a traditionally male area, the shift to a product has significantly changed the relationship between the club and the fan. It is evident how Campbell's theory operates here. The football club becomes invested with a mythical quality, drawn from the fans' 'daydreams'. These dreams can then be exploited by their commodification. The difficulty comes when the consumer is faced with the stark reality of business, consumption and profit seeking, as was the case during the takeover of Manchester United Football Club by the Glazer family from the US in 2005. Fans protested and some formed a breakaway club, which began the season in the North West Counties League. This example shows that Miles' (1998) assertion has validity: the ideological reality of consumption (profit and exploitation) is usually hidden (or ignored). The association of sport, consumption and identity is contained in a short piece by Taylor (2006, pp 18-19), who, in describing his new-found allegiance to Manchester United, writes that he does not know "if he is a United fan anymore", given that he now watches and supports the non-league team. His identity as a 'fan', once unquestionable, is now in doubt.

Edwards' (1997) study of male fashion argues that consumption offers opportunities for self-expression, which is open to everyone. Despite this apparent benign exterior, however, the reality is that consumption is far from 'democratic' (1997, p 134). Firat's work on the commodification of the male body (1994) and Mort's (1996) study of the more flexible styles associated with the rise of the 'new man' show how male culture (whatever that is or was) has become subject to the demands of the marketplace and consumption. This has developed further with the notion of 'metro-sexuality', embodied by David Beckham, a "top-class footballer, [who] wears sarongs and nail varnish and changes his hairstyle more often than most women" (*Western Mail*, 2003). While this market survey showed that most men had as their idol the actor Sean Connery, a significant number opted for Beckham. Metro-sexuality was defined as "straight men who know and care about fashion, food, and good grooming, and don't care who knows it" (Kirsch, 2003).

Clarke and Critcher (1985) argue that leisure is increasingly dominated by commercial interests. The examples given show just how far this becomes the case. It confirms their assertion that in work time, people are exploited by producers; in leisure time, business exploits people through consumption.

Consumption and the excluded

There are three main points to be made at this stage, and these will be explored more fully in the next chapter. First, consumption can be a vehicle by which some 'excluded' groups achieve inclusion. A prime example here, already hinted at above, is that of gay men. The evidence suggests that gay men are more likely to be found in the major cities of London, Manchester and Brighton and that they are more likely to be in higher socioeconomic groups. Whether the pink pound is a myth or a reality, gay people have been targeted as a specific consumer group (Burston, 2003). Millward (2005) reported on moves to 'sell' cars to gay men and that the Smart Car had been voted 'gay car of the year'. Gay tourism, according to a report by Majendie (2006), is worth around £3 billion a year to the UK's economy. A report by Curtis in 2006 noted that the value of the so-called pink pound had reached an estimated £70 billion. The editor of one of the magazines involved in this survey indicated that leading UK brands were re-evaluating their products and strategies to improve their 'gay market positioning'.

Not all gay people are rich with high disposable incomes, however, and it is not the intention to suggest that gay people do not face prejudice and discrimination. The evidence indicates that capitalism has seen a potential market and seeks to exploit it. In this regard, consumption acts as a mechanism for a type of economic inclusion, even if only in the sense that exploitation does not discriminate in terms of sexual orientation.

Equally, black and minority ethnic groups have increasingly been subject to the attention of the consumer society. Ojumu (2004) reported that the black pound was worth about £32 billion each year, although minority ethnic groups were among the last to be specifically targeted (after the elderly's 'grey pound' and the pink pound). Allan Leighton, chair of the business organisation Race for Opportunity, told the BBC that his organisation was "interested in business understanding if you are good at race then you'll make more money" (BBC News, 2005).

Thus, if there is significant disposable income, previously excluded groups can be included because of their patterns of consumption. Following Campbell's analysis, the wonder is that it took so long: all people consume and we all have dreams. Indeed, it could even be suggested that those who experience forms of social exclusion are more likely to feel dissatisfaction, and therefore be more likely to consume. The urbanised nature of the consumption of gay people and black and minority ethnic groups tends to confirm an early assertion by Simmel (1950) that the contemporary city and urban life have ceased to be sites of production and have become those of consumption.

The second point is that consumption itself both creates and compounds certain forms of exclusion. Gabriel and Lang (1995) argue that the main barrier to participation in the consumer society is lack of money. So, like other social mechanisms located within a market economy, consumption can exclude just as much as it can include. If someone lacks the money, their patterns of consumption are limited. If there are certain products or items that someone does not possess, a likely consequence is a feeling of shame and exclusion. If we think of consumption as identity, the full impact of this form of social exclusion cannot be readily dismissed as an advertisers' 'con-trick'. It may be, but it represents reality for many people.

Third, one of the key writers in relation to consumption and the poor is Bauman (2000, 2005). Bauman offers a postmodernist interpretation and argues that consumption is the driving force behind the Western economy, and as such has replaced production. When production dominated, the poor were low-skilled and low-paid wage labourers, but nonetheless they had a use and a role. Now that production has been replaced, the poor are little more than 'flawed' consumers. With their traditional role in industrial capitalism as a reserve army of labour removed, they serve no real purpose. Their sense of inadequacy stems not from a lack of esteem brought about by unemployment, but rather by their failure to consume, and thereby to participate fully in a consumer society. Thus, poverty remains, but the personal meanings attached to it have changed.

Of course, there is a whole range of shops that target those with less income, including young people, a significant proportion of whom are, as we are constantly reminded, students.

Bauman's claims need caution, since production is still important in considering consumption. Clarke and Critcher saw this as an exploitative relationship. The work of McRobbie (1997) in relation to gender is of further significance here. She argues that the fashion industry targets women as the consumers of fashion, and that the sociological accounts of consumption focus on aspects of meaning and style. By using the fashion industry as an example, McRobbie argues that for many poorer women, this style is unattainable and therefore excluding. Further, she argues that the women who are the producers of these clothes (as opposed to the designers or models) are themselves usually the recipients of low wages, whether in the UK or further afield. Thus, the link between production and consumption is confirmed.

There is one major growth area of consumption that has been left until last, since it is an area that directly concerns social welfare professionals: the consumption of care. Older people, physically disabled people, learning disabled people and people experiencing chronic mental ill health are all significant consumers of care and social services, whether they be delivered through health, education or social care departments. For social workers and their service users, this has been a considerable change, and it is this that will be explored in the next chapter.

Note

[1] Miles' insistence on linking theory to the real world has been a source of inspiration to the authors who then began to explore areas, in which they already had an interest, by relating them to the study of contemporary society.

EIGHT

Social work: the power of consumption and the creation of customers

This chapter uses case studies to highlight the consequences of being unable to consume, the increased isolation experienced by many families and individuals, and how this affects social work. It concludes with an examination of how social work itself has become an enterprise based on consumption, arguing that for many people choice is but an illusion.

Case study 1

"I work with families who are poor. They don't have very much money at all and I think life is a constant struggle for them. Most of the families are single mothers and I think they really suffer. I mean, they can't get out themselves very much – some of the teenage mums long to go shopping for clothes but they don't go much further than the cheap high street shops, because they know they can't afford it. They feel really bad that they can't get their kids computers, iPods and things like that, unless their own parents will buy it. Most of them go into debt at Christmas, just to make sure they have a good time ... some of the families I know have debts to loan sharks, and of course paying the money back is a problem."

Social worker, area-based childcare team

Case study 2

"He's really into this type of music, I don't understand it. It gives him something he can identify with. He's out with his mates, hanging around, I know, but they just want to be on their own and they don't get into bother. But he wants the clothes that go with the image."

Mother of 14-year-old boy

Case study 3

"How many times do I have to give social workers the same information? Each one asks the same type of question and they all get the same answer, because there is only so much that you can say. I've had this for 20 years or so, social workers asking the same questions ... always assuming that they have turned up in the first place. I still do not know what is available, and they are always assessing ... what I want is some security for my son and somewhere he can live with a degree of independence. In the end, I know it will all come down to money, and who can get what resource."

Mother of a young man with a 'severe' learning disability

Case study 4

"The new systems are all well and good. They do provide a level of individual services, which wasn't always there in the past. There is also a degree of clarity and transparency in the assessment process; after all, every social worker has to complete the same form, whatever can be said, it is a standardised process. When the needs are identified we then have to identify a provider from the voluntary or private sector. The problems can start then; the service user has no one to effectively complain to."

Social worker, adults' services team

These case studies represent many areas social workers deal with (see also the case studies in Chapter Six). Consumption and the consumer society are relatively new developments, as demonstrated in Chapter Seven. It is, however, important that social workers make some attempt to understand how they affect the lives of people they work with. Readers are invited to return to the exercise in Chapter Seven to reassess the extent to which consumption plays a part in their life. It may be that it plays a far bigger role than at first thought.

This chapter will also show that the concepts of production and consumption are closely related, and the areas discussed lead to a consideration of the extent to which contemporary society has shifted to consumption and whether production still plays a significant role.

Consumption and exclusion: service users, poverty and debt

Chapter Seven developed the ideas of Bauman in relation to the 'new poor'. His argument is that they are the flawed consumers of a postmodern or postproduction world, and as such serve little purpose, as their traditional position as a reserve army of cheap, casualised labour has been eroded (Bauman, 1998). This view of the poor in relation to consumption is not without its critics. Byrne (2002) draws attention to two pieces of evidence to counter this view. This first is that many of the poor are poor because of low wages and it is this that determines their economic position. Second, he identifies the obvious: there is a range of shops that target the poor with cheap products. Low-paid work is the growth area of the economy, and this, according to Byrne, cannot be lightly dismissed. He concludes that production still matters in determining who is and who is not 'poor'. The economy needs the consumer power of the poor, and the existence of high street stores and large supermarket chains that sell cheap clothes shows this. Of course, we are not suggesting that only the poor shop there, but it is fairly certain that the poor do not shop at exclusive stores such as Harvey Nichols or buy state-of-the-art Bang and Olufson music systems – not even from eBay, an internet auction site.

For social workers, the relationship between service users and consumption may appear to be rather vague when compared with either production or reproduction. One of the areas where the effects can be clearly seen, however, is in the relationship between service users and debt. The extent of personal debt in the UK is currently around £15,000 per person, according to a BBC radio news report (BBC, 2006). This is close to what is regarded as the 'mean income', although the average wage (before tax) is somewhat higher. More importantly, Phipps and Hopwood Road (2006) found that the average debt of clients consulting the Citizens Advice Bureau (CAB) is £13,153 and that over half of clients are in receipt of incomes that are half the national average (that is, less than £11,000 per year). A spokesperson for the CAB commented that:

> Low income, combined with badly informed and poorly understood financial decisions, are at the root of many of our clients' debt problems.... The reality is that they are condemned to a lifetime of poverty overshadowed by an inescapable burden of unpayable debt. (CAB, 2006)

The debt is fuelled by credit-card and store-card spending, which is attractive to those on lower incomes, and this is another feature of a society based on consumption. Money becomes something that is 'sold'. Advertisements frequently refer to 'loan sales' by banks and finance companies offering lower interest rates; they are, in effect, selling the consumer money at a low rate of interest. Another feature of this for poorer people is that it is harder for them to secure 'low-cost' loans, and this can lead to borrowing from loan sharks. At a national lobbying conference on poverty and debt in 2003, a delegate known only as Sheila (her name was changed) gave an account of her experience of debt. Hers was a family where both partners worked and as a result found obtaining loans relatively easy. The debts they incurred came from moving house and buying new furniture. She later discovered that her husband had incurred more debts and that he had been abusing the children, resulting in a court case:

> "Eventually I had to give up. I could not make ends meet. My daughter brought me to my senses, when I discovered her feet were swollen from wearing tight shoes as she did not want to worry me by asking for new shoes that I could not afford to buy her." (Church Action on Poverty Debt Lobby, 2003)

She said of her experience of loan sharks and debt collectors:

> "I went to college and they followed me there and asked for my new
> address to call for the money owed. I will never, as long as I live, rely
> on moneylenders or companies that charge extortionate rates of
> interest. [A shop in Glasgow] offers a bed (advertised in Argos for
> £199) for £299, which, with interest payments, comes to nearly
> £800. How can they get away with this? They are parasites feeding
> on the fact that credit is hard to get if you are staying on this estate or
> unemployed." (Church Action on Poverty Debt Lobby, 2003)

In Birmingham, where there is a pilot Loan Shark Team, which seeks to identify
and prosecute 'loan sharks', a man was recently found guilty of charging his
customers interest rates of 1,000%. The trial revealed that he had worked for a
loan company and when he left he took the details of people who had been
refused loans. The loans he made were for relatively small amounts, but the
repayments were high. A typical loan of £100 would generate repayments of up
to £1,000 in total. Perhaps somewhat surprisingly, his sentence was 150 hours'
community service (BBC News, 2006).

The pressure of a society where there is an abundance of consumer goods on
offer, coupled with the accessibility of loans, potentially creates difficulties for
many of the poor, who are rendered even more vulnerable by the high rates of
interest they may be forced into paying. Credit Unions are a viable alternative
for many poorer people. Each Credit Union is built around a 'common bond',
usually determined by place or employment and they are financial cooperatives
owned and controlled by their members. Members can save and then borrow at
generally low rates of interest and for many poor people they are a way to access
money for essential purchases without paying high rates of interest (see
www.abcul.coop).

Before leaving the theme of debt, it is important to point out that debt is not
simply the preserve of the poor. It is likely to be an experience shared by both
social workers and their service users, although the level of debt and the ability
to repay it may be different. The point is to highlight the ubiquity of debt and
how, as has often been commented on, the early 21st-century consumer boom
in the UK has been funded by borrowed money (Haurant, 2006; Stewart, 2006).
It could be argued that the origins of debt arguably lie in the nature of the late
capitalist, post-industrial economy, although there has been a tendency to blame
poor people for their debts (Murray, 1984). It is relatively easy to locate debt
within a framework of individual fault and character weakness, and to render the
structural problem a personal one. One of the social worker's enduring dilemmas
resurfaces: personal or structural failings? The authors suggest that debt is endemic
and is encouraged to fuel economic prosperity, and that this is a structural question,
deeply entrenched within the economy and one that affects most people at least

some of the time. The poor are, however, the most vulnerable and there is a further paradox. Consumption is also a means of inclusion, as Chapter Seven demonstrated. By chasing this type of social inclusion, the vulnerability of the poor leaves them more likely to end up socially excluded.

Consumption as identity: we are what we consume – the impact on the 'new poor'

Chapter Seven showed the importance of consumption in creating and sustaining forms of identity through lifestyle, leisure and culture. Identity has been on the social work agenda for some time and is usually viewed as part of its psychological or psychodynamic tradition; as such it is part of social work's 'casework' history (Perlman, 1972). In the 1980s, there was renewed focus on identity, especially among black children, many of whom had been fostered by white families (Fahlberg, 1994). Other developments in identity have been concerned with the concept of life histories and life-story work for children and young people in care, but these are largely located within the theoretical discipline of (social) psychology (Sutton, 2000). Earlier chapters introduced the importance of work in giving people a sense of identity and purpose, and the next section develops the themes of identity within a community. The importance of groups and peer relationships, especially in relation to youth culture, should not be underestimated, and many of these emanate from sociological studies (Parker, 1974). Finally, the growing importance of ethnicity, and also particularly Islam, as a form of identity cannot be ignored, nor can its relationship to patterns of wider discrimination and exclusion (Centre for Contemporary Cultural Studies, 1982). Social work has often adopted a sociological analysis here, but equally sees it as part of 'religion and culture' shaped by traditional ethnic identity (see 1989 Children Act).

Applying the material from the previous chapter, identity can be formed and sustained by factors that are not only external to the individual, but also not directly based on personal relationships. Therefore, a study of consumption opens up a new reality that identity can be sought, created and sustained through commodities, and the outward signs of belonging to a particular 'culture' (Miles, 2000). The importance of this for younger people cannot be overstated. Young people whose families lack income are likely to experience aspects of exclusion by their school peers if they cannot fully identify with particular youth cultures. By their nature, these are simultaneously both inclusive and exclusive. It could well be argued that the young person who wants expensive, branded trainers is not just succumbing to the pressures of advertising. It is rather that the advertising creates a particular image and identity and it is this that the young person wants to buy into (Lunt and Livingstone, 1992). It is all too easy to dismiss this, but the impact can be considerable on young people who experience multiple exclusions due to their poverty (Ridge, 2002).

This is an area that is underplayed in much social work literature. The impact of poverty is clear, but all too often its consequences in terms of identity are overlooked. It may even be the case that not being able to buy into one particular identity may lead to others being chosen, which create a sense of belonging but have negative results. It is interesting, though not surprising, to note that working-class culture, or cultures connected with the poor, are often derided. The development of the so-called 'chav' culture, which copied the clothing of wealthy celebrities, with fake jewellery and Burberry clothes (an expensive brand), created a form of identity. The 'chav' has been identified as either working class or as part of an 'underclass', although it could be argued that chavs are just another aspect of subcultural groups (Harris, 2006). It is the desire to mimic wealthy people that has led to much of the criticism – perhaps an example of the poor being blamed for their own poverty, while those with wealth can create trends that are then 'marketed' for others to follow.

Ultimately, social work should not dismiss the issue of an economically created and sustained identity among the groups it deals with. These identities have meanings for the individuals concerned, in the same way that for other generations being a mod, a rocker, a hippy or a punk had the same relevance. Once again, it has a resonance across all groups and for all people; who among us has not been part of, or on the fringes of, some subcultural group?

Social work as consumption: the business of social work and the creation of 'service consumers'

The application of consumption for service users may be just a more up-to-date version of an impact of poverty upon people's lives. The most interesting application of the concept is in relation to the nature of social work and welfare services and their relationships with the people they serve. It is here that we can begin to see how concepts of production, reproduction and consumption are brought together in the provision of contemporary social services in the UK.

Harris (2003) developed the argument that social work had become a business in his book *The Social Work Business*. He suggests that whereas social work began as service provision, a combination of business practices and a focus on service user choice has significantly altered the nature of how services are provided and delivered. The significance of Harris's work is that it locates social work within an economic and political context, of which, it could be argued, consumerism is the latest 'phase'. His argument here rests firmly on the notion that before the business era – in the period up to the early to mid-1980s – social work was part of a social democratic state, and that accountability was through the political process (MacDonald and Jones, 2000). Market forces played virtually no part in social work at this point and the social work professional had a degree of autonomy (Friedman, 1977). The establishment of social work as a business is a central feature of the Griffiths Report (1988), which went on to form the basis of the 1990 NHS and Community Care Act, the establishment of a quasi-market in social welfare and the development of a new discourse built around the ideas of the so-called 'purchaser–provider' split (Le Grand, 1990). Local authorities became the purchasers of services, but their role as providers was gradually weakened and taken over by the voluntary and private sectors. This was based on the idea that a multiplicity of providers would result in competition and therefore drive down costs and possibly increase choice. To achieve this, principles of management theory were to be introduced to ensure the establishment of a new set of ideas and principles (Harris, 2003, pp 44-55).

The language of the new business is one of personalised services, with the concepts 'needs-led' and 'tailor-made' dominating the agenda. The service user or, as Harris argues, the 'new customer', has the right to have their individual needs assessed, and for personalised services to be provided. Choice has come to dominate the agenda of social services departments, and the recipients of services are consumers rather than clients or service users. The concept of choice provides challenges for social work staff and service users alike. One study has shown that of all public services it is social work's staff and service users who are the most positive about the move towards consumerism (Clarke, 2004; Clarke et al, 2005). The same survey also gave a clear warning about such systems, in that around one in five workers and users saw the potential for those who had either the skills or the loudest voice to gain disproportionately. Significantly, less than 5% of either staff or service users wanted to be seen as 'customers' or 'consumers', with the majority preferring to be either members of the local community (41%) or service users (35%). The project, undertaken in 2003-05, identified that while public services are constructed on consumerist lines, the majority of the people who use them have little identification with the term 'consumer' or even 'citizen':

> Customer implies you toddle in, and you look at various things and you toddle off if you don't fancy it. Or you demand the most expensive, perhaps. (Clarke et al, 2005)

The conclusion drawn is that while service users want good individual treatment and choice, equity matters and the choice agenda renders decision-making processes less, rather than more, transparent. The public appears to be more concerned with quality of services, confirming Barnes and Prior's (1995) findings.

Case study 3 highlights another aspect of the move towards the consumerist approach. Harris makes the point early in his text, when he describes the experience of trying to organise services for his father and being asked the same questions by three social workers. He concludes:

> These three social workers have taken me through a scripted assessment over the telephone. I have had scripted exchanges that were more

engaging and responsive at the windows of drive through fast-food restaurants. (Harris, 2003, p 2)

This is the business approach, which seeks to standardise assessment under the guise of 'needs-led' services. It is a consequence of managerialism (Clarke and Newman, 1997), yet it is still undertaken by social work staff. More concerning is the view that, by offering 'needs-led' services and promoting choice in this way, service users are being 'empowered'. Indeed, it would seem to be a common thread in undergraduate social work responses that by giving choice, they are behaving in a way that 'challenges' negative systems. The reality is, however, that little choice is being offered, and in any event such practices actually underpin a market economy that has often rendered those same service users poor and excluded in the first place. This reflects a trend first identified by Jones and Novak (1993), where social workers are regulated and thereby services are controlled according to available resources. In summary, social work decisions are reduced to financial decisions. Within the world of consumption, this was summarised by Fine and Leopold (2001, p 17):

> The notion of value for money extracts the essence of the supposed condensing of social relations into the world of consumption, making explicit its association with the purchase of commodities, irrespective of what explicit values are used to assess 'value for money'.

This locates the trend towards consumption of public services within a distinctly free-market agenda and highlights that it then underpins social relationships. The more pertinent question is, to what extent has choice actually been promoted? For, if the changes have truly brought about 'tailor-made services', the dilemmas of formulaic responses may be worthwhile.

The consumers of social services are mostly people who are poor and lack the resources and information to be what Warde (1994) describes as 'competent consumers', not least because consumers of social services do not have the ability to substitute an inferior product with a superior one. The language of consumption obscures the relationship to the economy of service provision. By creating an illusion of the poor service user as a 'customer', the reality of economic and political rationing is hidden (Fabriquant and Burghardt, 1992; Lewis and Glennerster, 1996). More significantly, consumer welfare goes further: it implies consensus where there is potential conflict (Mouffe, 2000), it denies emotional contact between the social worker and the service user, and ascribes a false 'equality' between service user and social worker through a contractual fallacy, ultimately masking the "social relations of welfare" (Hoggett, 2000, p 152). Direct payments, introduced to provide greater levels of independence for people needing care, may not even be the answer, even though many welcome them as providing service users with far greater control over their care (Glasby and Littlechild,

2002). First, however, this reduces the caring relationship to one based on cash value alone; in short, it turns it into a commodity. Second, it implies an unfounded faith in the ability of market forces to deliver (Barnes, 1997). Thus, for vulnerable people with complex needs, this could be little more than shifting the burden of risk from the state to the individual, and turns collective questions into personal ones (Esping-Andersen, 2002).

White and Harris (2001, 2004) suggest that for service users the shift towards a social welfare system based on consumption has brought some gains; but it could be said that these are largely offset by the deficits identified above. For the impact of the changes on social workers, we return to themes of production. They have been reduced to offering standardised 'needs-led' assessments that do little to 'individualise' needs. Jordan with Jordan (2000, p 23) argue that service users or customers:

> ... end up queuing for commodities which are strictly rationed by the authorities according to their own criteria of risk and need, and then being given something which does not fit or suit and is certainly not chosen.

The social worker appears caught between a rhetoric of choice and the reality of limited options. Limited options have always been a feature of social work, but previously within a social democratic context (Harris, 2003). Furthermore, the social worker has been subject to workplace regulation and has been turned from a 'professional', or at least semi-professional (Etzioni, 1971), into a proletarianised worker. The principles of factory organisation now apply to social services; indeed, borrowing from Ritzer (1993), the standardisation process has almost resulted in the 'MacDonaldisation' of service assessments (see Chapter Four).

The final section of this chapter shows how the shift to consumption has helped create new categories of production, thus making the sociological circle complete. The shift away from local authorities as major, even monopoly, providers has resulted in the proliferation of voluntary and private sector services. While some of these demand high skill levels, many provide a social care workforce that is relatively low skilled, low waged and female (Littlewood, 2004). This is a new arena of low-paid work, drawing on a casualised and feminised workforce, and one that underpins the nature of contemporary care provision. In effect, care has become an aspect of production.

The major consumers of care are those who are vulnerable: older people, people with disabilities and especially people with learning disabilities. The very people who are among the casualties of contemporary society have created a new arena of production. The low-paid nature of the job of caring for these people, however, confirms not only their status – indeed, it took a government White Paper in 2001 to make valuing learning disabled people a central and named policy objective – but also the financial value placed on the caring role. Informal care is promoted as being both desirable and usual. While carers are officially recognised, this is also a feature of the shift towards consumption and a move away from the social democratic ideals of welfare, as indicated above. The caring role is seen as being natural (Ungerson, 1987), to the extent that Birmingham Social Services Department's assessment forms ask the carer which caring roles they undertake, what information or training they need to undertake these roles, and what other commitments they may have, including work. Never are they asked whether they *want* to care. Caring is regarded as a privatised matter, and only in the absence of family carers is it commodified and made a public matter.

The social care workforce, mainly women and employed in the voluntary sector on low, often minimum, wages, is one of the consequences of a move away from the social democratic ideal towards the economic politics of choice. It has created a class of casual labourers who are women. The chapter now returns to the themes of production as outlined in the first section. The nature of contemporary society is one that is based on the continued exploitation of workers, with poor conditions of service, often fitting their work around their own domestic arrangements. It is therefore here, at the very heart of contemporary social work and social welfare, that the sociological and economic themes of the book converge, in the demonstration of the interplay between consumption, reproduction and production.

Before exploring concepts of community and responses to it, it is important to consider whether service provision, which turns the service user into a 'customer', actually affects social exclusion. Chapter Seven drew on material that suggested that consumption could act as a force for inclusion, for example, in relation to the 'pink pound'. Since consumption is premised on large corporations needing people to spend their money, then we can see how we are all included as potential customers, with 'consumer rights'.

There are two points to make here. First, while the poor are not just Bauman's 'flawed consumers', for they are specifically targeted as consumers, the key factor in people's ability to consume is their level of income. Without the money, consumption is limited or else driven and funded by debt.

Second, in relation to social work, does the move towards consumerism actually benefit the 'customer' in reducing their levels of exclusion? The overwhelming majority of the users of social services are poor and/or socially excluded (Barry and Hallett, 1998; Gordon et al, 2000; Jones, 2001). The type of services provided may promote inclusion: the experience of direct payments may, for some, promote greater autonomy (Glasby and Littlechild, 2002) but the manner in which they are provided will leave many people in the same situation as before. The move towards 'consumerism' is a further twist towards individualising social work practice and moving away from collective solutions. By supporting the illusion that we are all equal as consumers, social workers are in danger of masking the existing levels of exclusion, poverty and inequality that the people they work with experience. Consumption may act as a motor for inclusion, but in doing so it masks inequality and exclusion, and creates yet another tension within capitalism, with which social workers have to contend.

Part Five
Community

NINE

A changing landscape: theoretical approaches to 'community'

Having explored the factors that provide the economic base of contemporary society, and how these explain social exclusion and affect people's 'life realities', this chapter explores the nature of community. It provides a brief overview of core theories in the study of community and argues that the traditional community based on proximity to work and family ties is disappearing as society becomes increasingly fragmented and people alienated. As the subsequent chapter demonstrates, this has potentially serious consequences for social work.

What do we mean by community?

Activity

When you hear the word community, what do you think of?

Most people, most of the time, think of community as being about people and places. Generally, it is the idea of place that defines community; indeed, official documents often embody this idea of community. Of course, people are essential to the idea of community, for we talk about a community of people living together, occupying the same space and also having something more in common. As a concept, community has become increasingly widespread in its use, and it is suggested here that all too often it is used without a full exploration of its meaning. As with many words, the assumption is that we all know its meaning and what it conveys. The sociological analyses, however, show that community is a changing and contested concept.

More complicated than you think: sociological theories old and new

When examining community, Cree (2000) suggests that the term can be characterised in three ways: locality, social networks and relationships (which, in this case, transcend locality). The difficulty for sociologists when considering community is that it is virtually impossible to think about community *without* networks and relationships. What is of paramount importance is the type of emphasis given to these three components in the sociological accounts. After all, it is people who make up communities, and wherever there are people there will always be some form of relationship between them – even if this is strained. A fourth category could be added to those defined by Cree: community as 'discourse', which will be explored later in the chapter.

Activity

Which types of community do you belong to? How often are you referred to as being 'part of' a specific community?

First, it is important to note that whatever community means to individuals, it is experienced differently according to age, gender, sexuality and ethnicity. How readers respond to the questions above will, of course, depend on many factors, but it is likely that most people would have identified some aspect of place. This might be a strong identification with an area of a town or city, or a smaller rural village. Within this place, there would also be connections with other people who share a similar socioeconomic or class position. This might also be extended to include a broader locality: someone who lives in Wolverhampton may have a strong identity with the city and there may also be a sense of local antipathy to neighbouring towns. This antipathy, however, could be constrained by an all-embracing identity with the region, known as the 'Black Country'. This will be different according to where you live: someone from North London may see themselves as different to someone from the East End, yet they can both celebrate their identity as Londoners.

It need not stop there. You might belong to a community that celebrates a particular ethnic identity. This might be connected to where you live, since often people who share a similar ethnic background live in the same area. You can belong to the community and not share a locality; for example, you could be an 'exiled' national, typified by the many people of Scottish, Welsh and Irish origins who live in England, let alone those of overseas nationalities. A further consideration may be religion and a sense of belonging to a faith-based community. For some, there would be a sense of belonging to a political party or some other local/national organisation. Community is defined as a shared interest and can readily transcend place. You could see yourself as part of a football team's fan community. Indeed, as teams style themselves more as 'brands', there seems to be a paradoxical attempt to create a sense of shared community among supporters who do not live in the same country, let alone the same city.

Your answer to the questions above might also depend on your age. It is likely that the older you are, the more you will think about what community used to mean. The shift away from production towards consumption has significantly changed the way that community is conceptualised. It seems to have weakened the sense of shared space and place, and emphasised ideas and identities within an increasingly individuated society. The sociologies of community will now be explored in greater detail, paying some attention to the power of community to *include* and, potentially, *exclude*.

Social relationships: traditional communities and the industrial city

The German sociologist Tönnies, writing in 1887 (Harris, 2001), was one of the first to examine the nature of community and society, and the idea of community organised around locality or neighbourhood can be traced back to his analysis. Tönnies used the term *Gemeinschaft* to refer to a community in a clearly defined locality, where people had interdependent relationships. The German word has its root in *Gemeinde*, which can be translated into English as parish. The essence of this type of community is that it is an 'ideal type' based on three ideas: bonds of kinship or family; mind, that is, being with other people who share similar ideas; and land, that is, a long-standing connection to a place. Tönnies argued that it was not the rise of industrialisation that led to the breakdown of traditional society, but rather that society was already breaking down and this in turn created the conditions for industrialisation to flourish. The connection with Durkheim's ideas of mechanical solidarity (see Chapter Three) are striking.

For Tönnies, this type of community had been in decline for many years. So, the culturally homogeneous society, regulated by a shared moral, religious and familial code that led to high levels of social cohesion, had been in decline, allowing for the development of capitalism and industrialisation.

Tönnies saw modern society as characterised by *Gesellschaft*, a word still used to refer to 'society'. The growth of the city brought benefits, but it also fundamentally changed the way in which people related to each other. Tönnies argued that social relationships were conducted on an individually contracted, or rational, basis, rather than being based on traditional norms and, to use a more current term, values. Industrial society was more mobile and this in turn led to social relationships that were more impersonal and transient (Simmel, 1971). Accordingly, people invested less time in these relationships, making deliberate and rational calculations about them. At this point, Tönnies' argument becomes more complicated. He does not say that the old, traditional community has merely been replaced by the impersonal city, but that within the city, new forms of *Gemeinschaft* develop (Harris, 2001).

Tönnies' theory about community is highly significant and quite durable. It identifies key aspects of community that have been developed by other sociologists but it also has a strong emphasis on the *relational* aspects of community and society and how these are, and have been, affected by capitalist development. In this way, it does not necessarily have to be seen as a pessimistic, or even socially conservative, theory that charts the inevitable decline of community, since it offers the potential for people to create meaningful social relationships within different contexts.

Studies of working-class communities in the 20th century tend to confirm Tönnies' basic premise here, demonstrating that to see modern society in terms of a *Gemeinschaft–Gesellschaft* distinction is, in fact, a false dichotomy. Young and Willmott's (1957) study of Bethnal Green is a good example. The expectation of the study was that postwar reconstruction would have brought about a breakdown of community, whereas the reverse was true, with high levels of homogeneity and stability identified. Bell (1968) studied a middle-class housing estate in Swansea and discovered that kinship ties can be maintained even over long distances, whereas Bulmer (1987) shows that similar patterns affect working-class communities and that friendship bonds have replaced kinship bonds as being important on a daily basis.

One of the crucial, yet often overlooked, aspects of community is how it exerts a level of control over its members. Within traditional communities, this control is less 'rational'. However, as will become apparent, not all aspects of control that emanate from communities in the 20th/21st-century UK can be seen as rational. What seems to be significant here is that when people live together in communities where the bonds are clearly discernible, there is likely to be a greater sense of collective loyalty, unity and something that can be called 'morality'. Habermas (1998, p 4) argues that "the morality of community not only lays down how its members should act: it also provides grounds for the consensual resolution of conflicts". It is this aspect of the traditional community that seems to be 'lost' in contemporary society, but what can also be seen is that it can equally be identified and potentially recreated.

Cities and urban communities: relationships and identity?

Modern society is not bounded by place in the same way as Tönnies' *Gemeinschaft*, nor is it rooted in a set of traditional social bonds, and cities are often associated with the decline of community. Drawing on aspects of Durkheim's theory of anomie, the American sociologist Wirth (1938) argued that the city completely destroyed any sense of 'organic' society. Cities are lonely places, with only fleeting 'human' relationships and this is compounded by large populations. There is a tendency for cities to be socially divisive, accentuating the gap between rich and poor, as reflected in the neighbourhoods people live in. Wirth echoes another of Durkheim's themes about modern society: it offers both the potential for greater freedom and choice, but at the same time increases instability and insecurity. Faced with this, Wirth argues, people need to find some form of neighbourhood-based association to try to recreate their 'lost' stability.

Gans (1968, in Bocock et al, 1980), in a later response to Wirth, sees cities as relatively stable places. He identifies two groups: 'the cosmopolites' and the unmarried or childless who choose to live there; a third group the 'ethnic villagers' who live there by either necessity or tradition; and finally two groups who live in the city because they have no choice – 'the deprived' and the 'downwardly mobile' (p 400). Gans predicts the regeneration and even gentrification of many of the UK's large cities: areas that were previously either undesirable or left desolate have been redeveloped, often with expensive apartment-style accommodation. He also notes how there are significant student populations in cities, which give them an added vibrancy and cosmopolitan feel. There is a suggestion here that the development of cities can extend 'freedom' without an attendant loss of social interaction. Indeed, it is possible to argue that one reading of Gans could imply that for some people traditional communities can be both stifling and 'excluding'.

These studies have given rise to sociological debates about the nature of modern living, which tend to place much less emphasis on place and far more on relationships. Calhoun (1998, p 381) argues that:

> Community life can be understood as the life people live in dense, multiplex, relatively autonomous networks of social relationships. Community life thus, is not a place or simply a small-scale population aggregate, but a mode of relating, viable in extent.

What he is arguing here is that the enduring feature of community is how people relate to each other. This might once have been straightforwardly based on kinship; in modern society, these relationships are more complex and often separate from family. Indeed, the internet and subsequent developments in technology have given a new meaning to the term community. It is possible to develop real-time relationships with people you have never seen, in places you have never visited, through internet chat rooms. It is also possible to follow a particular interest from a distance and be joined with others who share the same interest. Thus viable communities of shared interests are developing through the use of technology.

Castells (2001, p 127) sums this up and also sets out what it could mean for community:

> ... to understand the new forms of social interaction in the Age of the Internet is to build on a definition of community, de-emphasising its cultural component, emphasising its supportive role to individuals and families, and de-linking its social existence.

This is a significant development, for it suggests that community can be determined by shared ideas that transcend place and traditional notions of what a community might mean. On the one hand, there is the positive potential that it can offer viable and valuable support to individuals and families, but what it underlines quite clearly is that it removes people from a social existence. Thus, the conclusion is that for community to have a sense of the social, it must be located in how people form and sustain social relationships in relation to social space (Evans and Fraser, 1996).

Ethnicity is a key factor in the creation of urban communities. Gans identified the ethnic village, and this is also explored in a well-known study of Sparkbrook in Birmingham by Rex and Moore (1967). Dench and colleagues (2006) explore the conflicts that have emerged in communities around race. They repeat Young and Willmott's (1957) original study and suggest that it is, in part, the housing policies of the welfare state that have contributed to a weakening of kinship ties and fuelled racism and conflict in the new East End, although there is a similarity between the views of older Bangladeshis and white families regarding newcomers.

Ethnicity, however, provides a strong sense of belonging. Many of the UK's cities have neighbourhoods where ethnic groups have developed a clear sense of identity, whether this be Tower Hamlets in the East End of London for the Bangladeshi community or Digbeth in Birmingham, a focal point for the city's Irish community. One of the features that emerge is the recreation of a *specific* form of ethnicity. It is the case that very often the second or third generation rejects the policies of integration followed by the parent first-generation migrants. This complex phenomenon demonstrates the dynamic nature of culture. Jacoby (1999, p 48) argues that ethnic pluralism can often derive from integrated communities "who are re-inventing the long lost roots of their grandparents: 'what the son wishes to forget, the grandson wishes to remember'". In this sense the urban community serves as a source of identity and also offers the potential for a shared moral code.

The sociological studies of urban communities and communities in the technological age emphasise aspects of choice and flexibility around relationships and social arrangements. In many neoliberal societies, 'choice' has become the clear mantra and driver of social, economic and political change. In relation to community, however, how far can people make choices about where they live and with whom they interact?

Community: inclusion or exclusion?

The extent of choice is one of the themes to have emerged from the sociological study of contemporary society and the implication in more recent writings about community is that it can be applied here as well. This chapter now explores to what extent this has been and is the case, especially in relation to whether community serves to *include* or *exclude* people.

Many studies focus on the inclusive nature of community and the importance of social relationships in sustaining this. Studies also reveal that there is an aspect of exclusion attached to community. Not only does the concept have a variety of definitions, but it also has at its heart another aspect of dualism and dialectic.

It has already been noted that experiences of community depend on gender, ethnicity, age and sexuality, and to that can be added the notion of class.

Gans (1968) concluded that the way of life followed in the city has more to do with social class and lifecycle than location. He noted the existence of those who are poor and also trapped: people who have no control over where they live. Rex and Moore (1967) observed that it was no accident that different groups occupied different types of housing; this was largely determined by allocation policies (during the 1960s, there was a substantial stock of public sector housing administered by councils). The ability to buy can now be added to the equation. For most people, where you live is determined by what you can afford, not where you choose to live. Thus, choice is severely constrained.

Another factor of urban living is the differential access to transport. Many cities in the UK have relatively poorly developed transport systems. As a result, many people rely heavily on cars. This is an area where the concepts of consumption and community intersect. The poor are frequently excluded from car ownership. This is not simply because of the cost of buying a car, but also because of the cost of running a car. Although car ownership at a national level appears high, the figures are inflated because richer households often own more than one car. In cases where poorer people own cars, the vehicles are usually older and more unreliable. For Froud and colleagues (2005), the car reflects the narcissistic, self-interested consumer. In an earlier work, Sheller and Urry (2000) discussed the relationship between the developing city and the car. Although their study was based on the US, recent UK trends confirm its findings. It begins with exploring the different meanings car ownership has for men and women, which the authors of this book see as being linked to the commodification of desires and Campbell's work on consumption. Significantly, though, Sheller and Urry see the car as transforming city life, dominating its design and establishing the superiority of car users over others. Thus, the city becomes a place that is not person-friendly and is dominated by the car, which is an extension of the expression of identity, style, gender and class through consumption.

Other studies of the city reveal it to be a place of fear and danger (Davis, 1999). This leads to differential outcomes, which can be observed in most UK cities. The rich can afford to live in well-appointed areas of the city, either in the suburbs, in gentrified city centres, or even in 'gated communities', cut off and separately policed from the rest of the city. Levels of crime in cities are highest in areas of deprivation: those who experience crime are likely to be poorer (ONS, 2003) and also from BME groups (Salisbury and Upson, 2004). The danger is that such concerns are translated into concerns about whole communities (Harvey, 1973) and that, especially in relation to crime, certain groups are pathologised and stereotyped. Thus, African Caribbean males are seen in a certain way, primarily as perpetrators of crime, even though they are more likely to be victims of crime than young white males (Smith, 1997). Images of the city, particularly certain areas of the city, as dangerous persist, and, indeed, many areas of cities *are* dangerous places. The question is whether this is based on individual pathology or whether it reflects wider social inequalities. This takes us back to one of the tensions in social work: do we seek individual or structural explanations? Giddens (1982) was clear that capitalism had affected both the development of the city and rural society, and that people's lives are shaped by labour, *not* where they live. It is the relationship to production that ultimately shapes the nature of community, and the shape community takes will be either inclusive or excluding.

Exploring the nature of the city reveals much of this to be self-evident. The greater the level of affluence, the greater the choice over where you live. Thus, it may be that a relatively wealthy person may choose to live in a relatively poor area of a city, but for most of the people who occupy that area there will have been no choice. In many studies of traditional working-class communities, location was determined by production. Seabrook (1978) tends to have a romanticised view of the working-class community, with strong bonds to family and location. Fulcher and Scott (1999) point to the fact that the forces of production in themselves encouraged strong communities, and again this calls into question whether industrialisation led to the decline of community or was caused by it. In fact, it could be argued that the decline of a traditional working-class community, based on a lifetime in the same job with strong trades union solidarity and local support, is also in decline as the nature of modern capitalism changes. The demise of traditional industry in certain parts of the UK has significantly altered the nature of community and examples can be seen in the former pit villages and towns of South Yorkshire and South Wales, the latter being the site of some of Europe's most deprived communities in the early 21st century (David and Blewitt, 2003).

In an interview with Barry Hines about his South Yorkshire heritage, Richard Benson discusses the nature of a community based on production. There is a sense of nostalgia for a time that has disappeared, which Hines acknowledges is romanticised:

> "The people who made those things and designed them were proud of them. I mean, most of the blokes in Sheffield who worked in the steel factories were proud. You would be, if you were walking down the street in Brighton or somewhere and you saw 'Made in Sheffield'. You'd say, 'Look at that! I made that' or 'So and so made that'. Or 'We did that'." (Benson, 2005)

The wife of a former miner reveals the nature of nostalgia:

> "You've to be careful you don't look back with rose-tinted glasses, you know", she says. "There was definitely less crime because we all knew each other, but then again there was everyone knowing all your business. We appreciated what we had more then, but we're

more prosperous now. We've got more material things, it's just that there seems to be less ... communication, somehow." (Benson, 2005)

These two extracts can be used to demonstrate benefits, but also losses, that have come with the demise of production. They also hint at the potentially claustrophobic and exclusionary nature of a community where everyone 'knew your business'. Nevertheless, shared location and work generated a community that seems to be firmly located in the past. Communities based on the reality of production also had a clearer understanding of power. Sennet (1977) develops the idea that a focus on community at the expense of structural factors effectively masks the nature of power in society. He foresaw a danger in the individualised world of late capitalism, which allowed the power of capital to go unchecked. The paradox is that as the trend for more local and individual power and autonomy gathers apace, the actual sources of power are removed from view:

> ... the belief in direct human relations on an intimate scale has seduced us from converting our understanding of the realities of power into guides for our own political behaviour. The result is that the forces of domination or inequity remain unchallenged. (Sennet, 1977, p 339)

The idea that communities have a pathology that stands outside the structural nature of society can also be seen in ethnic communities, where there is an increasing emphasis on cultural identity. Such communities are created and sustained by common experiences of social exclusion and discrimination, alongside the need to create sets of organisations that can act as a defence against racism. Castells (1997) argues that these are communities of resistance, where ethnicity is combined with religion, nation or place. Individuals seek collective identity within the community, rejecting ideas of individualism.

An emphasis on 'culture', particularly where it is reduced to religious difference, can mask the nature of power imbalances. For example, references to unemployment and poverty in the 'Islamic' community in the UK come from the reality that the group of people who experience the greatest levels of poverty in the UK are Paskistanis and Bangladeshis. As we have indicated earlier, the poverty of this group does not stem from their religious beliefs but is a *structural* division based on class, evidenced by poverty and extreme disadvantage.

The inclusive nature of old-style communities appears to have disappeared, but although inclusion was strong, so was the potential to exclude. Tightly knit urban communities can serve these purposes just as well. Nor should the potential for conflict within a locality or neighbourhood (community as locality) be lightly dismissed. Communities can be in conflict or tensions between community groups may be triggered by a specific incident that feeds into long and deeply held antipathies. Community, therefore, can be a place of conflict and tension, especially as new groups try to establish themselves and their own cultures (Park, 1952; Fischer, 1999).

Community as discourse

Community encompasses a variety of meanings and, despite some of the negative aspects identified above, there is little doubt that it is used invariably with a set of positive overtones. When the word community enters the discourse, it is usually seen as a 'good thing'. It suggests unity, harmony, cohesion and a set of common or shared interests – a true utopia.

There is a genuine discourse that has grown around this almost uncritical acceptance of the essential 'goodness' of community, particularly in relation to social work. As has been noted, however, it is also a term that is used to promote aspects of consumption and generate 'brand' loyalty. There is a clear paradox, however. Not only is community often the site of tension and conflict, but communities in the traditional sense are also disappearing:

> Never was the word community used more indiscriminately and emptily than in the decades when communities in the sociological sense became hard to find in real life. (Hobsbawm, 1994, p 428)

Did such communities ever really exist? An early study by Stacey (1960) showed that external forces exerted pressure on traditional communities. She questioned the extent to which any true belonging actually existed, even when people had long histories in the town. Moore's (1974) study on Durham mining towns and villages showed that, despite a similarity of place, people's loyalties lay in religious or political groupings, often at odds with each other. A later study in Scotland (Moore, 1982) showed that it was self-interest, rather than group solidarity, that prevailed and created divisions within the community. Other studies point to the particular role of women in maintaining a sense of community (Williams, 1997), underlining gender differences located within the division of labour, for example.

Benson's interviews in Yorkshire (2005) offer a slightly different perspective: such communities did exist, but they were not necessarily the ideal they appear to be from a distance of years. Hobsbawm, however, strikes the right note when he stresses the indiscriminate use of community and links this to an apparent nostalgia for this bygone age. Hobsbawm, too, would be referring to communities based on production and doubtless bounded by place, rather like the Yorkshire pit village.

Bauman, from his postmodern position, associates the yearning for community with a sense of lost security. This echoes the Durkheimian concept that the human condition is essentially 'social' and not individual, and that the drive among social beings is for collective living, which gives rise to a sense (real or imagined) of security. Durkheim (2002) notes that a lack of stability in society leads to unstable personal lives. Bauman sees the postmodern society as being increasingly individuated and the isolation that can result leads to greater levels of insecurity. The paradox is that the individuated society offers the *potential* of consumer–based happiness, but its elusive quality leads to the demise of happiness that can be nostalgically claimed in the past:

> We miss community because we miss security, a quality crucial to a
> happy life, but one which the world we inhabit is ever less able to
> offer and ever more reluctant to promise. (Bauman, 2001, p 144)

Thus, the discourse of community conjures up a 'paradise lost' (Nisbet, 1967) and, however illusory this may have been, it is the *image* above all else that the discourse communicates. The ills of contemporary living are too easily blamed on lost community, and consequently the late 20th century saw a renewed interest in the concept. As Giddens (1994, p 124) argues, "on each side of the political spectrum today we see a fear of social disintegration and a call for the revival of community".

The next chapter examines the role of social work in this 'revival'.

TEN

Social work, social capital and community

The language of social work is 'community-focused' and 'community-based solutions' are sought. What does this really mean for social work practice and for those who live in communities? Is social work in fact retreating from communities, and distancing itself from exclusion and poverty? With a focus on choice, social work has succeeded in individualising social problems, yet offering little new in the way of solutions.

What is the meaning of social capital?

Social capital is difficult to define. It refers to those intangible resources: friendships, networks, trust and shared values, many of which are associated with positive ideas of community. Field (2003, p 1) sums it up as "relationships matter". This should have an immediate resonance for social workers who are engaged in a variety of neighbourhood-based schemes and projects.

Activity

To understand the importance of social capital, think about your friendships, the contact you have with your family and the extended networks of people you could call on to provide some level of support if needed. You could begin by thinking about the proximity of your family; the nature of your friendships and acquaintances; the organisations you belong to; and where you meet with other people of like mind.

Generally speaking, the more friends you have, the nearer your family and the greater your network of support, the greater your levels of social capital. The different types of 'community' you belong to can also reflect social capital. The sociological concept of social capital therefore provides a valuable framework for understanding the nature of community-oriented social work.

Social capital and class

Bourdieu (1984) is arguably the originator of the concept of social capital, which for him is closely aligned to cultural capital. This in turn is connected with consumption (see Chapter Seven). Bourdieu began with a study of French society influenced by class and he specifically investigated the French middle class. His interest is in how social capital (or the lack of it) is a feature in maintaining the existing social order and inequality. He also identified *cultural capital* and *actual capital* as being significant. In fact, his exploration of social capital followed these later. Bourdieu develops the view of social capital as being 'good' for the privileged, and being negative for the 'oppressed'. Social capital then becomes a mechanism by which certain social groups (usually those who already are privileged) maintain their power, status and influence. In contrast to later writers who have used the concept more positively, Bourdieu serves as a reminder that social capital preserves the status quo.

As Edwards and Foley (1997) argued, what Bourdieu demonstrates is that by preserving the position of the wealthy, social capital can serve to maintain social inequality. Other writers, however, have suggested that social capital can enable people to develop the necessary skills and supports to move out of poverty, especially when linked to benefiting from education.

Social capital and education

The American sociologist, Coleman, studied educational outcomes in relation to social capital and was influenced by 'rational choice' sociology. This assumes a highly individualised model of behaviour where everyone makes choices that serve their own and *no one else's* interests. Coleman (1990) confirmed that community was a source of social capital and that family or community supports outweigh those of the school. For Coleman, the main features of community and strong social capital are mutually reinforcing relations between people and institutions, which he called closure, stability and a shared ideology. The most effective types of community that generated this were 'small towns', where family and kinship are the most crucial factors. Coleman also saw religion as being important as it cut across the generational divide, and so in this way it could act as a kind of social cement, creating intergenerational solidarity. This work has resonances with Durkheim and also Tönnies. Coleman is optimistic that social capital can be a clear asset for social groups who are deprived, and is not just a mechanism for maintaining inequality. Coleman and colleagues' (1982) study, which focused on education, saw that children who went to Catholic schools in the US achieved better outcomes than children from 'public' (that is, state) schools, irrespective of their social background. He concluded that this was a consequence of strong community and parental emphasis on educational attainment, rather than the nature of the school per se. It is important to emphasise that within

Coleman's analysis of the concept, the central feature is self-interest; any sense of a collective is constructed out of mutual *self-interest* and not collective interests.

The study of social networks is an important adjunct to social capital and this has a longer history. The evidence generally points to improved outcomes in education, especially for the disadvantaged (Lauglo, 2000). Social networks – family and friends or a discernible 'community' – can be premised on a sense of *shared* interests, rather than self-interest.

Social capital, cohesion and civic engagement

While Coleman in the US and Bourdieu in France were arguably the originators of the concept of social capital, Putnam (2000a) has popularised it and is seen as its major proponent. His widely read book *Bowling Alone* (2000b) has popularised the concept. While Bourdieu and Coleman had a background in sociology and economics, Putnam was a political scientist, and his long-standing links with US governments afforded him a level of influence.

Putnam is interested in the concept of 'civic engagement' and the type of community that this creates. His theory, which is similar to Durkheim's ideas on social solidarity, sees social capital as developing from civic engagement, joining associations for the mutual benefit of everyone. This both 'bonds' people together and 'bridges' social divides. Kinship and family are not as important as social organisations. He describes the decline of volunteering and the joining of organisations as being symptomatic of a decline in social capital and society in general. Putnam identifies the following factors as being of considerable importance in the US, and they can be applied to the UK. The growth of two-career families mean people are too busy to give time to anything else. The expansion of the city has led to people travelling more since they live further away from their place of work. People's expectations have changed and there has been a growth in home-based entertainment (television, DVDs, computers, and so on).

His study also revealed a high correlation between social capital and positive outcomes in education, wealth, health and happiness. Whitehead and Diderichsen (2001) also demonstrate the benefits of social networks for health and well-being, with the mortality rates of those with high levels of social capital half of those with weak social ties. Thus, social capital has clear benefits for individuals. Maloney et al (2000) question whether civic engagement has been reduced to the same extent in the UK as in the US. Their study of engagement in Birmingham reveals an increase, especially if political engagement is included. A study by Surkemper (2003) reveals a decline in civic engagement in Germany, but nevertheless shows relatively high engagement compared with the US and the UK.

Putnam, unlike Coleman, also developed the argument that social capital generates reciprocity and trust. It is here that the links to Durkheim's sociology can most readily be discerned, for it is these factors that ultimately benefit the whole of society and act as a form of 'social glue'.

Finally, social capital can have its 'downside'. The nature of some of the social bonds that could be created and sustained could produce negative results, particularly in relation to race and segregated communities. We return to a theme of Bourdieu: social capital can maintain inequalities, and does not necessarily reduce them. If you do not share the group's values, the sanctions imposed (whatever their form) will be experienced in a negative way. The extent to which much of the American research develops a positive picture of social capital needs to be questioned. It has the power to exclude as well as include, just like community.

Social work and community

The origins of community-based work can be traced to the Victorian Settlements, which sought to integrate well-educated young people into working-class areas, aimed at bringing about better understanding between the classes, as well as improving the education and environment of the area (Briggs, 1976). They were established in many of the UK's large cities, in the late 19th century, the most well known being Toynbee Hall in London. The development of the St Vincent de Paul Society in Glasgow (see Chapter Two) is an early example of how social work responded to the specific needs of a migrant community, and, with a remarkable similarity to early 21st-century provision, this was often provided to migrants by those who shared their culture and faith. The community was one based on shared beliefs and values, yet at the same time it also served to cement those beliefs and values within the community, preserving them from possible dilution through integration. The early attempts at community work also involved those who would now be termed 'service users'; however, this was often out of necessity, as opposed to design, because there were no educated middle-class people to call upon (Anon, 1875).

In the UK, community work has a history of being seen as distinct from social work, and perhaps the high point of UK community work was the community development projects (CDPs) of the late 1960s and early 1970s. The origins of these lay in an attempt to prevent community breakdown and racial tensions (Loney, 1983). CDPs developed diverse approaches, but, as Loney noted, they were frequently at odds with official government policy. Another aim of the projects, and indeed of many community-oriented initiatives, was to help communities 'pull themselves up by their own bootstraps' (Crossman, 1977). Thus, communities were to help themselves. Mayo (1975a, 1975b) noted the potentially 'conservative' nature of community work, and aspects of this can be seen in a policy announcement by the UK Conservative Party in April 2006. It pledged to match the Labour Party's aim to eradicate child poverty by 2020 but the key to its approach was to build on community initiatives, involving the voluntary sector. This contrasts with a more 'top-down', state-led approach that focuses on aspects of wealth redistribution (Letwin, 2006).

Sure Start, a major government initiative developed by Labour in the late 1990s, aimed to reduce poverty in the short, medium and long term. Sure Start's aim is to assist in eradicating child poverty by creating supportive networks within deprived communities by mobilising a range of social work, education and healthcare resources. Key to the policy and the practice is enabling lone parents (mainly women) to enter the world of full-time employment and involving local people in service development (Glass, 1999). This demonstrates a close connection between developing social capital and encouraging an increase in 'actual' capital, by focusing on paid employment as a way out of poverty and deprivation. Another feature of Sure Start and similar projects is that of attempting to improve life chances through education. Here the links with social capital are clear: the better the level of education, the greater the employment potential. Social work, with its focus upon multi-agency working, is engaged in a number of ways with such activities.

First, there is the question of the educational attainment of some black and minority ethnic groups. Sewell (2000), a black academic and practitioner, has argued that while racism exists within the education system (see also Tomlinson, 2001), a significant factor is the lack of emphasis placed on educational attainment within black communities. He argues that only when this improves will the desire to achieve be such that the true potential of black youth will be attained (Sewell and Majors, 2001). This 'resistance' is located within the second and third generations, and, as Phillips (Press Association, 2005) has also noted, such a response actually throws away gains already made by black people. A focus on social capital here also goes some way to explain UK educational outcomes, where Indian and Chinese children do significantly better than other groups. Yet, on its own, it could be an individualisation of the problem. While intervention is focused on individuals, even communities, targeting what is perceived as 'dysfunction', the overarching structural inequalities that generate the feelings of resistance and alienation are ignored (Ferguson and Lavallette, 2004). The tension remains: improving educational outcomes for black youth can be a positive enterprise, but by such interventions it is very easy to imply that the 'problem' belongs to the individual and is not located within the structures of society.

Interventions here and with disadvantaged groups overall address structural inequality, although this is not explicitly stated. Educational outcomes are closely linked to social class (Reay, 2005). Thus, any attempt to improve these will also improve the condition of those in the working class. The language of the early 21st century denies the experience of class, and attempts to focus on social capital or 'community or cultural responses'; it thereby implies that a 'level playing field' already exists. Those who are routinely working with the poor and the socially excluded – including social workers – will know that this is most definitely not the case (Jones, 2001).

Second, the 2004 Children Act placed a clear responsibility on local authorities to improve the educational attainment of looked-after children. The educational attainment among this group of children is significantly below average (Conn, 2006b, 2006c). The Act is a rather belated attempt to improve the life chances of a specific group of children for whom the state acts as a parent (Conn, 2006a). Thus, social capital can have distinctly positive applications for social work practice, even though it does not remove the social worker from points of contradiction, since one objective of the legislation is to improve the *employment* prospects of looked-after children; aspects of regulation and control creep into the caring role. The policy is revealed to have an instrumental view of education. Nevertheless, an emphasis on education is overdue, necessary and, for those young people it targets, ultimately beneficial.

Third, social workers should ask themselves what they mean when they use the word community. It is especially useful to locate these questions in some of the theoretical approaches to community, outlined in Chapter Nine. Some of the uses can appear obvious, but they are less clear when more closely examined. The Asian community contains people from different countries and who hold different religious beliefs; the Muslim community may contain people who all share the same faith, but not necessarily the same country of origin, language or even the same form of Islam. It is from such considerations that postmodernist views have developed, with an emphasis on difference and diversity. As Garret (2002) argues, the move towards diversity has tended to ignore poverty, leading to a shift in focus of the social work agenda. Indeed, when examining the demographic evidence, the reality is that most ethnic minority communities are characterised by higher levels of poverty, deprivation and levels of alienation.

Finally, to return to the broader application and social work interventions with 'disadvantaged' communities, poverty and inequality are addressed by a focus on paid work and education. Yet, the interventions are targeted at those who are the existing 'victims' of an unequal system. By focusing on the poor and excluded, is there not an implication that they are to blame for their own situation?

Projects such as Sure Start will therefore promote a range of interventions to improve health and education, thereby seeking to address existing inequalities (McKnight et al, 2005). The need for such schemes brings together the concepts already discussed: the demise of traditional communities, brought about by changes in the nature of production, and the move towards a society driven by consumption. Strengthening families through work will serve to create the conditions by which society effectively reproduces itself; thus, all the essential theoretical sociological concepts come together in the development of social capital. The concept has very little currency among social workers and their practice, even though much social work activity seeks to promote network building, furthering supportive relationships and helping to build social capital. Encouraging people to become involved in community groups and organisations is also a way to increase their social capital.

Thus, we have another of social work's enduring tensions. Promoting social capital is a 'good thing', yet there is a sense in which it appears to offer not so much a route out of poverty, but, rather, more effective ways of managing it. We return to the tensions between 'care' – in this context, enhancing people's well-being – and 'control' – which sees the interventions as supporting forms of economic organisation that exploit people. Is the development of social capital merely another of those types of intervention that focus on the individual and either explicitly or implicitly suggest that the cause of their exclusion is the consequence of individual failings rather than structural factors?

Critics of social capital have demonstrated that it can be used in this manner. McClenaghan (2000) argues that a focus on social capital has become a viable policy option for those engaged in progressive welfare policy making. By focusing on social capital, attention is drawn away from inequality and poverty; that is, the lack of actual capital and financial resources. By focusing on building social capital, policies fail to engage with structural factors. Avis (2002) suggests that the concept operates within the arena of capitalist policy in general and thereby deflects from class inequalities, generated by capitalism. Given that the World Bank has commissioned a range of studies demonstrating the extent to which social capital can assist in the 'war on poverty' (Fernandez et al, 2000), perhaps the case is made.

Social workers also encourage the development of social capital in seeking to establish networks, often based on the notion of caring. Indeed, there is a whole swathe of UK policy based on 'care in the community' and building 'stronger communities'. Leadbetter (1997) noted that social capital helps build stronger communities and these are more able to look after themselves. Molyneux (2002) explores the underlying gender assumption within social capital and community, and argues that this holds back the advancement of women's rights.

Care in the community?

Social workers in the UK have been seeking 'community-based solutions' for many years. From the early closures of large-scale institutions, where large numbers of learning disabled and mentally ill people were 'warehoused', community has often been defined not by what it is, but rather by what it is not. In other words, *community* care is not *institutional* care. It is here that the idea of community holds considerable sway and is also closely related to notions of family, kinship and care (Fink, 2004).

In children's services, community support teams routinely keep children out of institutions and thereby in the community. The 1948 Children Act established the principle of 'prevention' in this context (Corby, 1993), but perhaps its most crucial application came in the 1980s with the large-scale closures of children's homes, reversing a lengthy postwar trend. An example of this was the report on the Community Homes Project (DHSS/ACCC, 1974) *Care and Treatment in a Planned Environment*, which outlined the proposals for Community Homes with

Education. These were purpose-built institutions intended to 'treat' the causes of delinquency before returning young people to their community, although, as Cooper (1969) noted, there was little point in this unless the communities themselves were also 'treated'. The 1980s saw a move away from institutional care, prompted by research into its effects and a general lack of efficacy (Millham et al, 1975). There was also a simultaneous critique of 'treatment' interventions with young offenders, which continued into the 1980s and targeted both treatment and custodial methods of dealing with young offenders (Rutter and Giller, 1983; Stewart and Tutt, 1987; Goldson, 2001). To see the move as being entirely driven by 'practice' would be to miss an important point: community options are generally cheaper, or at least they do not incur large capital investment in building infrastructure. Thus, community options become another way of saving money, but one that can lay some claim to 'good practice'.

Provision for older people has followed a similar trend. The 1980s and the beginning of a neoliberal economic agenda saw the closure of local authority residential homes and the opening of private care homes. These developments were brought to a head in the 1990 NHS and Community Care Act, which turned social workers into purchasers of care, usually provided by the private sector (Harris, 2003). From its inception, the legislation was seen to be contradictory: on the one hand, it offered possibilities for needs being better met, and, on the other hand, it was perceived to be underfunded, often leaving vulnerable people without services, or with reduced services. For older people, it meant a move towards providing them with care in their own homes – 'care in the community'.

There is strong evidence that this trend has led to such care being provided increasingly by family members or kinship networks, and that these carers are disproportionately women (Fink, 2004). Care remains a gendered occupation and even when the carers are not female family members, they are likely to be female and low-paid, and their labour often casualised. Here community intersects with reproduction and sustains a set of gendered assumptions (Williams, 1997; Dominelli, 2006). Wilson (1977) highlighted the role of women in welfare provision and Fink (2004) demonstrated that, in the intervening 25 years, little had changed in this regard.

For people who experience mental ill health, there has also been a move away from institutional provision towards community-based approaches (Beresford and Croft, 2004). The debate is marked by the contradiction between the need to care for the service user, and a perceived need to protect the public from potentially violent offenders. Rethink (2006) suggests that around 40 homicides a year are committed by people suffering mental ill health, with the perpetrator known to social services in half of these cases. By contrast, 300 people a year are killed as a result of drink or dangerous driving, and 100 women and 100 children are killed as a result of domestic violence. Thus, the focus on control is disproportionate, and the risks very small.

Not surprisingly, there have been similar trends in the area of disability, with the introduction of direct payments, monies paid directly to the service user to allow them to purchase their own care. Thus, the service user is no longer dependent on the local authority (or health service) to act as an intermediary. This has been the subject of long-standing debate and is seen as a positive development within the disability rights movement, yet others disagree and tensions remain (Glasby and Littlechild, 2002).

For people with learning disabilities, even where high levels of supervision are needed, the community is also seen as the solution, yet services are uneven in their distribution, and learning disabled adults often experience high levels of social exclusion, despite being 'integrated' into the community. Living in a house on a street with other people does not necessarily translate into a positive experience (Turning Point, 2004). Indeed, local newspapers often report residents' campaigns to close down small hostels for people with learning disabilities or mental ill health and ex-offenders.

In this type of service provision, community is seen as some kind of ideal, a world in which neighbours care for each other, and where families support their own. This is debatable, as has already been noted, but it is also clear that the nature of capitalist society is to help undermine the concept of community by its focus on the individual. Bauman (2001) notes increasing levels of individuation, something foreseen by Durkheim and Marx, from their different standpoints. As Bauman notes, the collective sense of community that people yearn for is something that has been lost. Interest in social capital from policy makers is a sign of this, but one that addresses the symptoms, not the causes.

There has also been an increase in 'village communities' or 'gated communities', which create separate enclaves for certain groups of people. Gated communities for the rich (Perea, 1996) are perceived to be an escape from the dangers of the city. There are also signs that the UK and Europe are following an American trend and building increasing numbers of retirement villages for older people. In a series of interviews in the *Guardian* newspaper, Angela Minton notes that in the US, Australia and New Zealand, retirement villages tend to be popular with the relatively affluent. They reflect the concept of the gated community and are exclusive and excluding. Not surprisingly, in the same series of interviews, the manager of a UK company that builds these villages supports them on the basis that they provide support and become a focal point for interaction. Finally, the interviews conclude with the chair of a housing trust, who supports the idea in principle as being one that offers support and choice, but points out that merely because people live side by side does not mean they interact (Graham, 2006).

Village communities for people with learning disabilities challenge understandings of what community, in relation to social work, actually means. While such communities are 'exclusive', in that they are built around the perceived needs of a particular group of people, they also provide what can be seen as a genuine 'community network', which is often missing for people who are 'integrated' (www.camphill.org.uk). Turning Point's report, *Hidden Lives* (2004), demonstrates the extent of social exclusion faced by people with learning disabilities in the community, where attitudes towards them remain negative, services are poor and their chances of work are very poor. This is not an argument for village communities per se; however, genuine integration seems a long way off, and social workers need to consider a wider definition of community, including that of finding friends and being accepted, rather than one that just seems to stress its non-institutional aspects. Turning Point (2004) points to poor public transport services and the poverty of learning disabled people, which add to their isolation and exclusion. As one support worker said, "there is no point living in the community if you are not able to be part of it" (Turning Point, 2004, pp 19-20).

Social work, therefore, appears to be chasing a lost ideal: there is an increased emphasis upon community within social work, at a time when the ways in which people relate to one another are being increasingly individualised and decreasingly collective. A consequence is that there is less tolerance of people and behaviour which appear to be outside the 'norm'. The dialectical paradox is that as many policies seek to highlight the potentially excluding nature of community, social work is seeking communities as a route to inclusion. In the UK during the early 21st century, there has been a focus on 'antisocial behaviour'. The police have new powers to seek out and punish those allegedly behaving in an antisocial manner, but far less has been done to address the causes of such behaviour. Efforts by the police to enforce these powers, aimed at preventing people from drinking alcohol in public places or congregating in large numbers, appear to be little more than attempts to control young people. This is part of a long tradition of fear of the 'delinquent youth' and, as Pearson (1983) graphically demonstrates, each generation has its particular 'respectable fear'. Cohen (1972) demonstrates how this can be generated into moral panic, resulting in the creation of 'folk devils' – be they 'mods', 'rockers' or the 'hoodies' of the present day.

Activity

In practice or on placement, think about how the concepts of 'community' or 'community services' are used in your place of work. As an exercise, you could record these and explore the different meanings attached to their usage. You can then begin to relate them to some of the theoretical concepts in Chapter Nine and possibly other chapters in this book and develop a response to the practice of social work/social care you are engaged in by considering the following questions:

In what way is community being used to enhance people's well-being? In what way is it being used as a mechanism to provide cheap levels of care and support?

Social work in the community?

If we accept the view that community is a location, it would be reasonable to expect social workers, working in communities, to share the same location. The idea of 'neighbourhood teams' has a lengthy history and they are premised on this concept of community being a bounded location. This idea for social work finds its origins in the Victorian Settlements (discussed earlier in the chapter) and enjoyed a revival in the 1970s with the advent of local authority reorganisation (Seebohm Report, 1968) and the CDPs. It was also an idea espoused by the radical social work movement in the 1970s (Hugman, 1977) and formed a central part of the largely ignored and neglected 'Barclay Report' (NISW, 1982). Indeed, the attraction of neighbourhood organisation was particularly strong in the 1980s, with support from both the political left and right (Jordan and Parton, 1983).

There are signs that local authority social workers are now being located away from the communities they serve. In the West Midlands, several local authorities have centralised their social work teams and closed local offices. The closures were often in areas of higher-than-average deprivation, with levels of vandalism a sign of the tensions within these areas. A retreat to central office may bring with it an element of safety, but it also dislocates social workers from the community, and they then have to drive into the area, assess for needs and drive back to their base. How much, then, do social workers actually know about the communities they work in?

The following, and final, section of this book aims to draw together the themes discussed and to argue for a social work practice that takes due heed of sociological explanations, offering suggestions as to how this can be incorporated into existing practice frameworks to enhance the quality of social work assessment and service provision.

Part Six
Transforming society:
social work and sociology

ELEVEN

Using sociology to inform practice

This chapter draws together the ideas of earlier chapters, arguing that the concepts discussed are interlinked and interdependent in relation to people's lives. They form the basis of the society in which social work operates. The question posed is whether social work has properly recognised the fundamental shifts in societal organisation and the increasing difficulties this brings for (potential) service users. Social work as an occupation is largely one of engagement with the poor, and this book has shown how poverty is endemic in our economic system and affects all service user groups. By exploring society though the concepts of production, reproduction, consumption and community, a sociological analysis has been used that focuses on the life worlds that service users, and crucially social workers, inhabit.

There is considerable continuity in the contradictory nature of social work. The book has also shown how society is changing because of the decline of large-scale production in the West, a shift to the service sector industry and an attendant decline in traditional communities. The economic system remains capitalist, although the way it manifests itself has changed. It has been suggested that it is the nature of consumption and choice that has come to be the dominant theme in this renewed version of market-driven capitalism. This has in turn created new challenges for social workers. Consumption creates the illusion of equality, masking the clearer inequalities associated with production.

The first part of this conclusion focuses on social work practice, and shows how sociology can inform all stages of intervention. This is arguably neither new nor radical, but it is a restatement of some of social work's traditional themes. It is heartening on the one hand to note that the *Framework for Assessment of Children in Need and their Families* is firmly linked to child poverty, and as such it is an acknowledgement from government that this is a significant area for social workers.

There are approximately 11 million children in England. It is estimated that over 4 million of them are living in families with less than half the average household income:

> Over the last generation, this has become a divided country. While most areas have benefited from rising living standards, the poorest neighbourhoods have tended to become more run down, more prone to crime, more cut off from the labour market. (SEU, 1998, in DH, 2000, p 1)

On the other hand, once poverty has been established, it virtually disappears from the document. Social work becomes a service industry, with its potential political nature removed. The book's final chapter deals with this more specifically, but for now it concentrates on the importance of incorporating sociological perspectives into practice. This is not merely a restatement of systemic approaches (Specht and Vickery, 1977) or even the more recently developed 'ecological approaches' (Jack, 1997). While these locate people within wider networks and in that sense are 'sociological', this book has emphasised the importance of a dialectical sociology as an analytical tool for understanding people's lives and experiences. There is a two-way relationship between economic and social structures in society and individuals, but it is the former that limits people's life chances, thereby creating and maintaining levels of inequality and social exclusion, and it is these themes that are placed centre stage by the nature of the sociological concepts drawn on.

Beginning with the community

Social workers, whether they provide services or undertake assessments, need to have a sound understanding of the nature of the locality and neighbourhood (community as place) as a prerequisite to understanding the nature of people's lives, as this short extract by a social worker illustrates:

> "I was allocated the case of a young single mother with a baby where there had been some concerns expressed about her care. I knew of the area [a large development of tower block flats to the south of the city] but hadn't really paid it much attention before. When I got there all the blocks looked the same, they were vandalised and the lifts didn't work. She lived on the fourth floor. The flat was OK, but as she said very early on in our discussion, she felt trapped. There was nowhere to go. Her companions were people on daytime television. Even though the flats were surrounded by greenery, it wasn't used as a park or communal area. There was nothing for children. I began to wonder. Here was a young woman in her teens, with a baby stuck in a flat. No wonder she was struggling. I have always gone back to the same question: how would I have coped?"

Without an exploration of what it was like to live in that part of the city – for example, the distance from the shops and the amount of effort needed to get there, the isolation of the tower block, the lack of public transport and the general isolation experienced – any assessment of need or risk would be partial. So, the place to begin is not with the individual as such, but the locality in which the person lives. A way of doing this is included in the following exercise.

Activity

Develop a profile of the community you work in. You can obtain a lot of information from the Census (the last one taken in the UK was in 2001 and this material can be accessed online at www.statistics.gov.uk). From this, you will be able to ascertain levels of poverty, the nature of housing and home ownership, the number of people in work and the breakdown of the population by age, gender and ethnicity. Statistical and demographic information is important but you will also need to know what it is like to live there. Walk about and see what it is like. What types of shop are there? What opportunities are there for entertainment? What is the housing like? What is public transport like? Where do the people who live there work?

This is the starting point of sociology in practice. It immediately locates the individual in their surroundings, and gives the social worker a good grasp of what it is like to live in that place, with limited resources. Such an approach involves using sociological knowledge and skills to improve practice and the lives of service users.

You can then begin to apply for yourself the concepts outlined in Chapter Nine and develop an understanding of the nature of the community the service user inhabits as well as the meaning of this for them. Community is not just about place, but also about the meanings that people attach to it. It could be that the nature of the community is supportive and provides a form of identity; alternatively, it could be the outward manifestation of a fully alienated society.

Understanding the importance of income: work, consumption and service users

The concepts of production (Part Two) and consumption (Part Four) are both, to a large degree, connected with the level of income people have and how they use their income. The significance of work is that it determines income levels. Without adequate income, many of the activities that can be taken for granted are not available. Many deprived communities do not have good transport links, and the people who live there lack work. This lack of work leads to reduced incomes and poverty, and results in diminished opportunities to partake in the consumer society. This forms a very powerful aspect of social exclusion and isolation. These forces all combine to produce a society where people experience high levels of alienation, through the interconnection of the concepts of production, reproduction and consumption.

Understanding the relationship between people and the economy is relatively straightforward. Exploring it within the context of the social work relationship needs some skill, if the social worker is to avoid appearing intrusive. The scripted interview is of little help here, for this would be at best factual. The need to maximise service users' income by ensuring full take-up of available benefits and local schemes (such as reduced entrance fees to leisure facilities) is still an integral part of the social work role, and one that would fit comfortably with existing assessment frameworks. In the authors' experience, however, it is an area where many social workers are not well informed and that is all too often seen by agencies as someone else's responsibility (Simpson, 2006).

The importance of work and consumption extends beyond income, however. They are also a source of self-worth, esteem and identity. Again, these are areas with which social workers have been traditionally engaged, but the nature of a sociological approach is that it locates these within structural factors, rather than personal psychology. Sociology therefore offers a series of explanations that locate people firmly within their localities and the structural nature of society, and in this way it moves beyond a potentially limiting, individualised approach. Remember, both work and consumption create and sustain personal identity. Of course, social work should be concerned with individuals but this must extend beyond a limited concern with the 'self' to a concern for all people and society.

One important area highlighted by the book is that of consumption and its relationship with style and identity. As has been noted, while this is related to poverty and exclusion, it is often ignored by social workers, or else placed into a non-sociological context. The importance of belonging, premised on style and even culture, has its roots in economic processes and should not be viewed solely as the preserve of 'psychology', 'tradition' or 'religion'. The forces at play are far more significant than that.

Understanding the nature of personal and social relationships: social work and reproduction

The first point here for the application of a sociological practice is to understand that social relationships have clear connections to other forms of society's structures. Social work, is routinely concerned with people's relationships, but deals with these in such a way as to dislocate them from society. Part Three of this book argues that a sociological imagination would be aware of how other forces – work, poverty, community and gender, for example – serve to structure personal relationships and affect them. The social worker's account at the beginning of this chapter illustrates this.

Much of social work practice, focusing on individual and family relationships, serves to support the workings of capital. This is the uncomfortable position that social workers have always had to deal with (Bailey and Brake, 1975; Corrigan and Leonard, 1978) and no apology is made for highlighting it again.

This is a complex area. The importance of relationships lies in their intimate nature, and as has been shown they can be a site of resistance. A sociological practice would not then reduce them to a crude economic determinism and dismiss them as false consciousness (Hall, 1988). However, they should not become the social worker's sole focus, nor should aspects of relationships be taken for granted. Careful attention to the detail of family relationships is essential; as has been shown, the family is also being subject to change, even though the discourse of family is as strong as ever. This, again, is part of the dialectic at work; it is the distinction between appearance and reality. The sociologies of change do require a personal 'consciousness raising' (Friere, 1970). Indeed, this is the centrepiece of Marxism, feminism and all sociologies of resistance and change: the personal *does* become the political, but the political should not be reduced to identity politics, divorced from structural factors (Sivananden, 2006).

Traditional, and even current, processes of assessment tend to focus on relationships and often seek individualised, psychological explanations for these. But does this give a full picture? The response offered here is that it is at best partial; at worst, it is in danger of blaming the victims. A sociological perspective might not provide all the answers, but it is part of the answer to the enduring tensions within social work practice.

Activity

In relation to your aspirations and ideas of what social work should be about, identify the tensions, contradictions and crises you face in your work. Examine these within the sociological context.

This exercise is the bridge to the final chapter. It is suggested that you apply this and think about it in relation to your work with service users and to the location of your work within your agency. Many social workers face greater pressures from social work *as work* than they do from assessments or service delivery. Frequently, this can be represented as an 'ethical dilemma', which the individual has to resolve. The authors suggest that the roots lie in what are essentially sociological and political analyses. Locating such difficulties within the personal sphere of ethics is another way in which appearance can mask reality.

Sociology enables us to pose questions and to move away from the relatively comfortable certainty of the personalised response to one that engages with structural factors. This includes the role of social work itself, and not just what social workers do.

Social work is inevitably concerned with people's well-being, and a sociological perspective will draw attention to the economic and social realities which have a negative impact upon this. By exploring key sociological concepts, we have shown that they have an immediate relevance for people's lives. In this regard they should be seen as essential social work theory, although all too often they are ignored for more individualised theories. Throughout the previous chapters we have shown that social work is beset by tensions and contradictions; in short, it stands in a dialectical position. Sociological perspectives will inevitably move the focus of social work interventions away from an uncritical focus upon the individual to establish an emphasis upon the nature of society. So, if the sociological perspective has any place it is in understanding the nature of crises and contradictions to bring about change. It is to this that the final chapter now turns.

TWELVE

Contradictions and change?

The previous chapter was designed to get readers thinking about how to use sociology in the work they undertake. Earlier chapters emphasised the material conditions of people's lives. We all experience the same things, but, of course, we experience them in different ways. How social workers apply sociological concepts to their work also depends on the kind of work they do, and where they do it. For example, some social workers are involved mainly in 'forensic' work, while others work in community settings. Some are 'providers', while others are primarily engaged in assessing for, purchasing or coordinating services.

This book also identifies that there is a lengthy tradition in social work that places social justice and change on the agenda. Students of social work want to bring about change, often expressed in terms of 'making a difference' (Price and Simpson, 2004). The changes to social work practice and organisation discussed in this book mean that this tradition is in danger of being lost. A consequence is that social work will become just another service industry. The authors' experience as educators also indicates that social workers want to reconnect with the lives of service users and communities: they do not enter the profession to spend their days filling in forms. They also realise that many of those who are involved in 'direct working' with service users are often low paid, relatively poorly trained and frequently perceive local authority social workers as distant figures.

With this in mind, the book concludes by examining this tradition of change in social work, realising that many things are far easier said than done. It is all very well to talk about collective action, yet social workers often work in situations where people are quite willing to complain, but less willing to engage in collective action to attempt change.

Transforming social work?

A theme of the book is that inequalities and poverty are explained at the economic level. By contrast, social work tends to work with individuals, so the first question is how to combine this with the concept of society. Is there, as Margaret Thatcher once said of society, "no such thing ... there are individual men and women and there are families" (Thatcher, 1987). When analysing social work practice this would often seem to be the case, yet the profession is called social work. The individualised nature of society is too frequently characterised by 'isolation' or 'social exclusion', stemming from self-alienation and society. This is the context of the book's concluding discussion.

It briefly explores the part social work itself has played in supporting or resisting post-1990 individualising trends. The authors' analysis and experience is that social work as a profession has at times pursued an agenda that has resulted in focusing on individuals at the expense of collectives. By collectives, we mean service user groups, sections of society that experience similar situations (for example, the poor and black and minority ethnic groups) and the ultimate collective entity, 'society'. It has already been suggested that an undue focus on sociologies of 'difference' may lead to losing sight of what people have in common and this helps sustain an economic system based on exploitation and inequality. Langan (1998) argues that in the 1980s social workers lost faith in the working class. There were also sociological and political attempts to create new alliances that transcended class (Rowbotham et al, 1979). If class was the driver of application of sociology to social work in the 1970s, by the late 1980s it had become diversity. The response was the development of anti-oppressive practice (AOP) (Braye and Preston-Shoot, 1995; Dalrymple and Burke, 1995), which emerged in the late 1980s, had its heyday in the early 1990s, and has continued in various guises to the early 21st century. AOP brought many positive developments for some service user groups, and to some extent offered the prospect of resisting social work's move towards technocratisation (Dominelli and Hoogveldt, 1996).

AOP was, however, a particular response at a particular time and one that fitted with a developing social work agenda shaped by the political forces of the free market. In his critique of the emerging process, Webb (1991) argued that it was the means by which the laissez-faire economic agenda would ultimately be perfected. This pointed to a lack of understanding of the specific political and economic forces that this book places central to sociological understanding. AOP has provided a sound basis for the incorporation of new social movements into social work, for example, the disability rights movement (Fagan and Lee, 1997), but this should not have been at the expense of other forms of social action and lobbying. Braye and Preston-Shoot (1995) saw AOP as being a development from radical social work and anti-discriminatory practice (ADP). AOP was seen as being 'revolutionary' and linked closely to ideas of political change, and it was incorporated into the social work agenda. A consequence of this was that students had to provide evidence of AOP in terms of their commitment to it and how it was incorporated into practice. In our experience as educators, what seems to have happened is that elements of AOP, identified by Braye and Preston-Shoot, have somehow been lost as social workers provide evidence of ADP and Biestek's social work values, which were criticised by AOP theorists as reformist or traditional (Braye and Preston-Shoot, 1995; Dalrymple and Burke, 1995). This does not mean, however, that those social workers do not aspire to a different type of practice and lack a commitment to these ideals.

Transforming society: dialectics and daily realities

At the beginning, this book outlined aspects of the dialectic and claimed that it often becomes lost in a language people cannot understand. It is a paradox that one of the most important aspects of both philosophy and sociology has become so obscured, and therefore the preserve only of those who can be bothered to find their way through difficult language. Subsequent chapters have attempted to identify areas where social workers face tensions and contradictions.

One of the daily realities for many social workers is that current social work practices turn vulnerable people into 'customers' with little actual choice. This appears as a needs-led approach, while the reality is that it loses the confidence of the people who use the service. Barnes and Prior (1995) argue that people want confidence in services, rather than choice, and that the social services customer is not a 'real' customer at all. They see them as 'proxy customers'; service users do not enter the social care marketplace by themselves, but it is the social worker who 'shops' on behalf of the 'service user'. Anyone who has ever shopped on the internet or by mail order knows what it is like to receive something that is different from what they thought it would be. For many service users, this is the reality of services. The difference is that they can neither exchange the goods nor obtain a refund. They should not be seen as Bauman's 'flawed consumers' but as 'captive consumers', with social workers acting as their 'proxies'. This is not a position of choice.

There is another observation about the apparent lack of contact in social work with those who are excluded that emanates from the authors' experience of teaching. Social work has a history of ensuring that it does not 'oppress' people and social work education has tried to challenge misconceptions about particular groups of people. In the preceding chapters, it can be seen how 'dominant discourses' often confirm negative and stereotypical views about people. If social workers do not routinely come into contact with people in their communities, the risk is that such challenges will remain abstract, and that preconceived ideas could remain.

So, what about the dialectic? Faced with a choice of sociological complexity disappearing into a sea of opaque, arcane language, we will try to keep it simple. Whenever there is a conflict between what you think you should do as a social worker and what you end up realising has to be done, the dialectic is at play. You have experienced a 'contradiction'; the fact that all your colleagues experience this contradiction could reveal a 'crisis' for social work. The point is not to brush these aside as being unprofessional, but to realise that these are the signs of the social work conscience, which may at times only flicker, but is nonetheless present (Husband, 1995).

In an article about culture that draws heavily on the sociology of Bourdieu, Houston (2002, p 154), argues that "Marxists do not do justice to 'agency' but are right in acknowledging the role played by capitalism by reproducing inequality within culture". His criticisms are in a muted form, but the dialectic is inextricably linked to agency and without human action it is nothing (Gramsci, 2003). At the heart of practice is the contradiction between individuals and the collective, the person and society. This book demonstrates that contemporary social work has become a service industry, overly concerned with individuals and frequently ignoring the effects and consequences of poverty and exclusion. Furthermore, this ignores all those people who never get assessed for services in the first instance. Many people do not approach social services, and large numbers of those do not get through the gatekeeping process and are turned away without a service.

While aspects of collective action have had a positive impact on services (Barnes et al, 1999; Beresford and Croft, 2004), the total fabric of society remains largely the same. The poor are still poor and still form the majority of service users. There is ample current anecdotal evidence that it is still those who 'know the system and can shout the loudest' who are likely to benefit the most.

Having a commitment to social justice was part of the nature of Victorian social work: it has been part of social work ever since. Sociology at its simplest points out the extent of inequality; at its more complex, it offers frameworks for action.

Transforming social work: a profession worth fighting for?

> In the past many people entered social work because it seemed to offer a way of earning a living that did not involve oppressing or exploiting people, but on the contrary could contribute, even in a small way, to social change. It was, in other words, an ethical career. That potential for social change has all but been squeezed out of social work by the drives towards marketisation and managerialism that have characterised the last decade and a half. Yet overwhelmingly it is still the case that people enter social work not to be care-managers or rationers of services or dispensers of community punishment but rather to make a positive contribution to the lives of poor and oppressed people. If it is the widening gap between promise and reality that breeds much of the current anger and frustration amongst social workers, it is also the awareness that social work could be much more than it is at present that leads many of us to hang on in there. (Jones et al, 2004, p 3)

In 2006, Chris Jones, a professor of social work, chaired a conference called 'A profession worth fighting for?'. It was closely linked to a social work manifesto (Jones et al, 2004) that calls for a new engaged practice striving for social justice. It argues that the current 'crisis' in social work is "a state of affairs that nobody in their right mind could possibly view as acceptable ... that budget dominated welfare systems are cruel and destructive of human well-being" and that there is a need for "collective organisation, both to defend a vision of social work based on social justice, and also to defend the working conditions that make that possible" (2004, p 1).

The daily difficulties faced by social workers who want to harness the forces of crisis and contradiction to create change, either in their profession or society, are identified here. The dialectic processes are apparent in the contradiction between appearance and reality, and between the demands placed on social workers and their fundamental desire to bring about change, or, in Reamer's (1993) view, improve the 'common good'.

Social work has to engage in workplace-based action to resist the rise of bureaucratic systems that make working for social justice difficult. Like Husband (1995), we accept some level of control is needed, since social work should not be an individualised, 'maverick' activity. Of Evans and Harris's (2004) argument that perhaps social workers have more 'discretion' than he had earlier thought, we are less sure, but are equally certain that social workers have to find ways of resisting further moves towards 'McDonaldisation' and begin to recover some of the ground already lost.

The lack of a campaigning voice in social work can be summed up by this extract from the British Association of Social Workers' (BASW) website, which recalls a speech made by a young Ukrainian social worker at the above conference:

> Here was a young woman wishing that perhaps in the future she could practise in a country where social workers are organised, united and are able to apply leverage, voice concerns or even influence policy. For me this brought home how little I perhaps use BASW. Here is an organisation providing everything Victoria so craved for and I simply take it for granted and let it be. Organisations like BASW can be powerful tools in aiding social workers but it needs my input, my support, me questioning policy and raising issues. (BASW North West region, 2006)

Chapter Eleven argued that sociology has an important place in informing practice and assessments. The conclusion is that sociology is important at two levels. First, it will enable social workers to make links between the nature of society, the people in it and the nature of social work practice. Second, it offers the prospect of change through action. This is easy to say, but not so easy to do. The authors recall an incident some years ago, when a social worker training at postgraduate level complained that engaging in AOP was not easy, because the employer did not want this to happen and did not allocate time for it. The nature of contemporary social work practice is by no means the most fertile ground for engaging in any type of radical practice; indeed, in many areas the prospect is severely limited. Yet, there is a contradiction here. The increasing work place regulation and controls could demonstrate to social workers how their dissatisfactions are, in reality, located within the experience of alienated labour. This experience of work may be a significant factor in any future radicalising of the workforce (Poulantzas, 1978).

Cree (1995, p 10) identifies part of the dialectical position of social work, arguing that "every new intervention in social work has been accompanied by both gains and losses, and consequences which are not always expected and predictable". The tensions of social work are best understood within a sociological language. The concept of the dialectic allows us to explore these tensions and to understand that they are an inevitable outcome of the contradictory position of social work in society. This does not make those tensions more bearable, but they can be eased by making alliances with other social workers and service users (Beresford, 2004; Jones et al, 2004).

The optimism that students have at the beginning of their programmes needs to be encouraged. Engaging with sociology is often a motivational factor: it confirms the reason for doing it in the first place. It is not the intention to extinguish that enthusiasm by ending the book on a negative note, but transformations come about by understanding why we are here in the first place. Nor is it the aim to make social workers feel guilty for not doing enough; the fact that they engage in a job that is often unjustly criticised is sufficient. So let us finish with this thought. There is an irony in the fact that organisations that claim to be promoting human welfare are perhaps unwittingly extinguishing the spark in their workers that is needed to promote human well-being at all levels. It is hoped that this book has made a contribution to keeping that spark alive.

References

ABCUL Credit Unions (2006) *Promoting Quality Credit Unions* (www.abcul.coop, accessed 11 November 2006).

Acheson, D. (1998) *Independent Inquiry into Inequalities and Health Report*, London: The Stationery Office.

Ackers, L. and Dwyer, P. (2002) *Senior Citizenship? Retirement, Migration and Welfare in the European Union*, Bristol: The Policy Press.

Adburgham, A. (1989) *Shops and Shopping: 1800–1914*, London: Barrie and Jenkins.

Aglietta, M. (1987) *A Theory of Capitalist Regulation. The US Experience*, London: Verso.

Allan, G. and Crowe, G. (2001) *Families, Households and Society*, Basingstoke: Palgrave Macmillan.

Anderson, B. (2000) *Doing the Dirty Work: The Global Politics of Domestic Labour*, London: Zed Books.

Anon (1875) 'Home Mission Work in the East of London', in J.R. Moore (ed) (1988) *Religion in Victorian Britain. Volume III. Sources*, Manchester: Manchester University Press.

Arber, S. and Ginn, J. (1990) 'The Meaning of Informal Care: Gender and the Contribution of Elderly People', *Ageing and Society*, vol 10, no 4, pp 429-54.

Argyle, M. (1991) *Cooperation: The Basis of Sociability*, London: Routledge.

Avis, J. (2002) 'Social Capital, Collective Intelligence and Expansive Learning: Thinking Through the Connections', *British Journal of Education Studies*, vol 50, no 3, pp 308-26.

Bagilhole, B. (1997) *Equal Opportunities and Social Policy*, London: Longman.

Bailey, R. and Brake, M. (eds) (1975) *Radical Social Work*, London: Edward Arnold.

Bailey, R. and Lee, P. (eds) (1982) *Theory and Practice in Social Work*, Oxford: Basil Blackwell Publishing.

Balakrishnan, A. (2006) 'Business Confidence in Germany Rises', *The Guardian*, 29 March.

Barnes, C., Mercer, G. and Shakespeare, T. (1999) *Exploring Disability: A Sociological Introduction*, Cambridge: Polity Press.

Barnes, H. and Baldwin, S. (1999) 'Social Security, Poverty and Disability', in J. Ditch (ed) *Introduction to Social Security*, London: Routledge.

Barnes, M. (1997) *Care, Communities and Citizens*, Harlow: Addison-Wesley Longman.

Barry, M. and Hallet, C. (eds) (1998) *Social Exclusion and Social Work: Issues of Theory, Policy and Practice*, Lyme Regis: Russell House Publishing.

Barnes, M. and Prior, D. (1995) 'Spoilt for Choice: How Consumerism can Disempower Service Users', *Public Money and Management*, vol 15, no 3, July–Sept, pp 53-9.

BASW North West region (2006) Untitled news contribution (www.basw.co.uk, accessed 8 June 2006).

Bauman, Z. (1998) *Work, Consumerism and the New Poor*, Buckingham: Open University Press.

Bauman, Z. (2000) *Liquid Modernity*, Cambridge: Polity Press.

Bauman, Z. (2001) *Community: Seeking Safety in and Insecure World*, Cambridge: Polity Press.

Bauman, Z. (2005) *Work, Consumerism and the New Poor* (2nd edn), Buckingham: Open University Press.

BBC News (2005) 'Diversity Good for Bottom Line' (http://news.bbc.co.uk/1/hi/uk/4626271.stm, accessed 27 June).

BBC (2006) 'Citizens Advice Report Warns that Many now Face a Lifetime of Debt', BBC Radio 4 *Today*, 24 May.

BBC News (2006) 'Loan Sharks 1000% Interest Scam' (http://news.bbc.co.uk/1/hi/england/west_midlands/4758637.stm, accessed 13 May 2006).

Beaumont, P.B. (1993) *Human Resource Management: Key Concepts and Skills*, London: Sage Publications.

Beckett, C. (2005) 'The Swedish Myth: The Corporal Punishment Ban and Child Death Statistics', *British Journal of Social Work*, vol 35, no 1, pp 125-38.

Beliappa, J. (1991) *Illness or Distress? Alternative Models of Mental Health*, London: Confederation of Indian Organisations (UK).

Bell, C. (1968) *Middle Class Families*, London: Routledge and Kegan Paul.

Bell, D. (1980) 'The Social Framework of the Information Society', in T. Forester (ed) *The Microelectronical Revolution. The Complete Guide to the New Technology and its Impact on Society*, Oxford: Blackwell Publishing, pp 500-49.

Benson, R. (2005) 'When we were Heroes', *The Observer*, 4 December.

Beresford, P. (2004) 'Striking Alliances', *Community Care*, 25 March 2004.

Beresford, P. and Croft, S. (2004) 'Service Users and Practitioners Reunited: The Key Component for Social Work Reform', *British Journal of Social Work*, vol 34, no 1, pp 53-68.

Biestek, F.P. (1961) *The Casework Relationship*, London: Allen and Unwin.

Blyth, E. and Milner, J. (1997) *Social Work with Children: The Educational Perspective*, London: Longman.

Bourdieu, P. (1984) *Distinction: A Social Critique of the Judgement of Taste*, London: Routledge and Kegan Paul.

Bowlby, J. (1953) *Child Care and the Growth of Love*, Harmondsworth: Penguin.

Bradbury, B. and Jäntti, M. (2001) 'Child Poverty across the Industrialised World: Evidence from the Luxembourg Income Study', in K. Vleminckx and T.M. Smeeding (eds) *Child Well-being, Child Poverty and Child Policy in Modern Nations: What do we Know?* Bristol: The Policy Press.

Bradshaw, J. (2003) 'How has the Notion of Social Exclusion Developed in the European Discourse', Paper presented at the Australian Social Policy Conference, Sydney, 10 July.

Brah, A. (2001) 'Reframing Europe: Gendered Racisms, Ethnicities and Nationalisms in Contemporary Western Europe', in J. Fink, G. Lewis and J. Clarke (eds) *Rethinking European Welfare*, London: Sage Publications.

Braye, S. and Preston-Shoot, M. (1995) *Empowering Practice in Social Care*, Buckingham: Open University Press.

Briggs, A. (1976) 'Social Welfare Past and Present', in A.H. Halsey (ed) *Traditions of Social Policy*, Oxford: Blackwell Publishing.

Britcher, D. (2004) 'Leeds United Season Review 2003-4: What Went Wrong' (www.mightyleeds.co.uk/seasons/200304part2.htm, accessed 31 January 2007).

Bulmer, M. (1987) *The Social Basis of Community Care*, London: Allen and Unwin.

Bunting, M. (2005) 'Consumer Capitalism is Making Us Ill: We Need a Therapy State', *The Guardian*, 5 December.

Burchardt, T. (2000a) 'Social Exclusion: Concepts and Evidence', in D. Gordon and P. Townsend (eds), *Breadline Europe. The Measurement of Poverty*, Bristol: The Policy Press, pp 385-406.

Burchardt, T. (2000b) *Enduring Economic Exclusion: Disabled People, Income and Work*, York: Joseph Rowntree Foundation.

Burchardt, T. (2003) *Being and Becoming: Social Exclusion and the Onset of Disability*, CASEreport 21, London: CASE.

Burston, P. (2003) 'Pink Pounded' (www.pinkfinance.com/c_contributors/c_p_burston_article_1.html, accessed 31 January 2007).

Bury, M. (1995) 'Ageing, Gender and Sociological Theory', in S. Arber and J. Ginn (eds) *Connecting Gender and Ageing: A Sociological Approach*, Buckingham: Open University Press.

Byrne, D. (2002) *Social Exclusion*, Buckingham: Open University Press.

CAB (Citizens Advice Bureau) (2006) 'Citizens Advice Report Warns that Many now Face a Lifetime of Debt', Citizens Advice Bureau Press Release, 25 April (www.citizensadvice.org.uk/index/pressoffice/press_index/press-060524, accessed 31 January 2007).

Calhoun, C. (1998) 'Community without Propinquity Revisited. Communications Technology and the Transformation of the Urban Public Sphere', *Sociological Inquiry*, vol 68, no 3, p 381.

Callender, C. (2003) 'Student Financial Support in Higher Education: Access and Exclusion', in M. Tight (ed) *Access and Exclusion: International Perspectives on Higher Education Research*, London: Elsevier Science.

Cameron, D. (2006) 'I Don't Believe in "Isms"', *Mail on Sunday*, 1 January.

Campbell, B. (1984) *Wigan Pier Revisited: Poverty and Politics in the Eighties*, London: Virago.

Campbell, C. (1987) *The Romantic Ethic and the Spirit of Modern Consumerism*, Cambridge: Polity Press.

Campbell, C. (1995) 'The Sociology of Consumption', in D. Miller (ed) *Acknowledging Consumption: A Review of New Studies*, London: Routledge.

Carabine, J. (ed) (2004) *Sexualities: Personal Lives and Social Policy*, Bristol: The Policy Press.

Carby, H.V. (1982) 'White Woman Listen: Black Feminism and the Boundaries of Sisterhood' in Centre for Contemporary Cultural Studies, *The Empire Strikes Back: Race and Racism in 1970s Britain*, London: Hutchinson Education.

Carpenter, M. (1968 [1851]) *Reformatory Schools: For the Children of the Perishing and Dangerous Classes and for Juvenile Offenders*, London: Woburn Press.

Carruthers, B. and Babb, S. (2000) *Economy/Society: Markets, Meanings and Social Structure*, Thousand Oaks, CA: Pine Forge Press.

Carvel, J. (2006) 'Third of Men Drink to Drown out Job Stress', *The Guardian*, 8 June.

Case Con Manifesto (undated) reprinted in H. Searing, *The Barefoot Social Worker* (www.radical.org.uk/barefoot/casecon.htm, accessed 14 November 2006).

Castells, M. (1996) *The Rise of the Network Society*, Oxford: Blackwell Publishing.

Castells, M. (1997) *The Power of Identity*, Oxford: Blackwell.

Castells, M. (2001) *The Internet Galaxy: Reflections on the Internet, Business and Society*, Oxford: Oxford University Press.

Castles, S. and Kosac, G. (1972) 'The Function of Labour Immigration in Western European Capitalism', *New Left Review*, vol 73, pp 3-21.

Centre for Contemporary Cultural Studies (1982) *The Empire Strikes Back: Race and Racism in 70s Britain*, London: Hutchinson, in association with the Centre for Contemporary Cultural Studies.

Chamberlayne, P., Rustin, R. and Wengraf, T. (2002) *Biography and Social Exclusion in Europe: Experiences and Life Journeys*, Bristol: The Policy Press.

Cheetham, J. (1972) *Social Work with Immigrants*, London: Routledge and Kegan Paul.

Church Action on Poverty Debt Lobby (2003) 'Sheila's Story' (www.church-poverty.org.uk/campaigns/Debt/my-life-in-debt, accessed 31 Jan 2007).

City of Coventry CDP (1975) 'CDP Final Report, Part 1. Coventry and Hillfields: Prosperity and Persistent Inequality', in M. Fitzgerald, P. Halmos, J. Muncie and D. Zeldin (eds) (1977) *Welfare in Action*, London and Henley: Routledge and Kegan Paul with The Open University.

Clarke, J. (1993) 'The Comfort of Strangers', in J. Clarke (ed) *A Crisis in Care: Challenges to Social Work*, London: Sage Publications.

Clarke, J. (2004) 'Creating Citizen Consumers: The Trajectory of an Identity', Paper presented at Centre for the Study of Commercial Activity Annual Conference, London, Ontario, 5-9 May (www.open.ac.uk/socialsciences/citizenconsumers/index.html, accessed 31 January 2007).

Clarke, J. and Critcher, C. (1985) *The Devil Makes Work: Leisure in Capitalist Britain*. Basingstoke: Macmillan.

Clarke, J. and Newman, J. (1997) *The Managerial State*, London: Sage Publications.

Clarke, J., Newman, J., Smith, N., Vidler, E. and Westmarland, L. (2005) 'Creating Citizen-Consumers: Changing Relationships and Identifications' (www.open.ac.uk/socialsciences/citizenconsumers/index.html).

Cohen, P. (1981) 'Policing the Working Class City', in M. Fitzgerald, G. McClelland and J. Pawson (eds) *Crime and Society: Readings in History and Theory*, London: Routledge and Kegan Paul.

Cohen, S. (1972) *Folk Devils and Moral Panics: Creation of Mods and Rockers*, London: Palladin.

Coleman, J.S. (1990) *Equality and Achievement in Education*, Boulder, CO: Westview Press.

Coleman, J.S., Hoffer, T. and Kilgore, S. (1982) *High School Achievement: Public, Catholic and Private Schools Compared*, New York, NY: Basic Books.

Conn, D. (2006a) 'Road to Nowhere', *The Guardain*, 5 April.

Conn, D. (2006b) 'Survival Tactics', *The Guardian*, 12 April.

Conn, D. (2006c) 'Threadbare Care', *The Guardian*, 19 April.

Cooper, J. (1969) 'Social Disadvantage and Social Help', *Approved Schools Gazette*, March, p 646.

Corby, B. (1993) *Child Abuse: Towards a Knowledge Base*, Buckingham: Open University Press.

Corrigan, P. and Leonard, P. (1978) *Social Work Practice under Capitalism: A Marxist Approach*, London: Macmillan.

Coulshed, V. (1988) *Social Work Practice: An Introduction*, London: Macmillan.

Craib, I. (1997) *Classical Social Theory: An Introduction to the Thought of Marx, Weber, Durkheim, and Simmel*, Oxford: Oxford University Press.

Cree, V.E. (1995) *From Public Streets to Private Lives: The Changing Task of Social Work*, Aldershot: Avebury.

Cree, V.E. (2000) *Sociology for Social Workers and Probation Officers*, London: Routledge.

Crossman, R. (1977) *Diaries of a Cabinet Minister, Vol 3*, London: Hamish Hamilton and Jonathan Cape.

Curtis, P. (2006) 'Gay Men Earn £10K more than National Average', *The Guardian*, 23 January.

Dahrendorf, R. (1959) *Class and Class Conflict in an Industrial Society*, London: Routledge and Kegan Paul.

Dalrymple, J. and Burke, B. (1995) *Anti-oppressive Practice*, Buckingham: Open University Press.

Daly, M. (2002) 'Care as a Good for Social Policy', *Journal of Social Policy*, vol 31, no 2, pp 251-70.

Daly, M. and Rake, K. (2003) *Gender and the Welfare State*, Cambridge: Polity Press.

David, R. and Blewitt, N. (2003) 'The Socio-economic Characteristics of the South Wales Valleys in a Broader Context: A Report for the Welsh Assembly Government' (www.wales.gov.uk/subiresearch/content/eru/projects/socio/pt1-e.pdf).

Davis, A. and Ellis, K. (1995) 'Enforced Altruism in Community Care', in R. Hugman and D. Smith (eds) (1995) *Ethical Issues in Social Work*, London: Routledge.

Davis, M. (1999) *Ecology of Fear: Los Angeles and the Imagination of Disaster*, London: Picador.

Davies, M. (1985) *The Essential Social Worker: A Guide to Positive Practice*, Aldershot: Gower.

Davies, M. (ed) (1991) *The Sociology of Social Work*, London: Routledge.

Day, P.R. (1987) *Sociology in Social Work Practice*, Basingstoke: Macmillan.

De Groot, G.J. (1996) *Blighty: British Society in the Era of the Great War*, London: Longman.

Dench, G., Gavron, K. and Young, M. (2006) *The New East End, Kinship Race and Conflict*, London: Profile Books.

Denham, D. (2004) 'Global and Local Influences on English Rugby League', *Sociology of Sport Journal*, vol 21, no 2, pp 206-19.

Denham, D. (2000) 'Modernism and Postmodernism in Professional Rugby League in England', *Sociology of Sport Journal*, vol 17, no 3, pp 275-94.

Denham, D. (2005) 'Marx, Durkheim and Weber on Market Society', Paper presented at 37th World Congress of the International Institute of Sociology, Stockholm, July.

DH (Department of Health) (2000) *Framework for the Assessment of Children in Need and their Families*, London: The Stationery Office.

DH (Department of Health) (2006) 'Social Care: Policy and Guidance' (www.dh.gov.uk/PolicyAndGuidance/HealthAndSocialCareTopics/SocialCare/fs/en).

DHSS/ACCC (Department of Health and Social Security/Advisory Council on Child Care) (1974) *Care and Treatment in a Planned Environment: A Report on the Community Homes Project*, London: Her Majesty's Stationery Office.

Dominelli, L. (1997) *Sociology for Social Work*, Basingstoke: Macmillan.

Dominelli, L. (1988) *Anti-racist Social Work: A Challenge for White Practitioners and Educators*, Basingstoke: Palgrave Macmillan.

Dominelli, L. (2006) *Women and Community Action*, Bristol: The Policy Press.

Dominelli, L. and Hoogveldt, A. (1996) 'Globalization and the Technocratization of Social Work', *Critical Social Policy*, vol 16, no 2, pp 45-62.

Dooghe, G. and Appleton, N. (1995) *Elderly Women in Europe: Choices and Challenges*, London: Anchor Housing.

Dorling, D. and Rees, P. (2003) 'A Nation Still Dividing: The British Census and Social Polarisation, 1971-2001', *Environment and Planning A*, vol 35, pp 1287-313.

Doyal, L. and Gough, I. (1991) *A Theory of Human Need*, London: Macmillan.

Durkheim, E. (2002 [1897]) *Suicide*, London: Routledge.

Durkheim E. (1984 [1893]) *The Division of Labour in Society*, Basingstoke: Macmillan.

Eberhardt, J.L. and Fiske, S.T. (eds) (1998) *Confronting Racism: The Problem and the Response*, Thousand Oaks, CA: Sage Publications.

Edwards, B. and Foley, M. (1997) 'Social Capital and the Political Economy of our Discontent', *American Behavioural Scientist*, vol 40, no 5, pp 669-78.

Edwards, T. (1997) *Men in the Mirror: Men's Fashion, Masculinity and Consumer Society*, London: Cassel.

Elchardus, M. and Cohen, J. (2004) 'Retirement as the Future of Work: An Empirical Analysis of Early Exit from the Labour Market in Belgium', in P. Littlewood, I. Glorieux and I. Jonsonn (eds), *The Future of Work in Europe*, Aldershot: Ashgate.

Engelke, E. (1996) 'Einführung: Studienreform in der Sozialen Arbeit – Ärgernis und Hoffnung', in E. Engelke *Soziale Arbeit als Ausbildung: Studienreform und -modelle*, Freiburg in Breisgau: Lambertus.

Engels, F. (1968) *The Origin of the Family, Private Property and the State*, New York, NY: International Publishers.

Englander, D. (1998) *Poverty and Poor Law Reform in 19th Century Britain 1834-1914: From Chadwick to Booth*, London: Pearson Education.

Erath, P. and Hämäläinen, J. (2001) 'Theory in Social Work', in A. Adams, P. Erath and S.M. Shardlow (eds) *Key Themes in European Social Work: Theory, Practice, Perspectives*, Lyme Regis: Russell House Publishing.

Esping-Andersen, G. (1990) *The Three Worlds of Welfare Capitalism*, Cambridge: Polity Press.

Esping-Andersen, G. (1999) *Social Foundation of Postindustrial Economies*, Oxford: Oxford University Press.

Esping-Anderson, G. (ed) (2002) *Why we Need a New Welfare State*, Oxford: Oxford University Press.

Etzioni, A. (1971) *A Comparative Analysis of Complex Organisations*, New York, NY: The Free Press.

European Foundation for the Improvement of Living and Working Conditions (1995) *Public Welfare Services and Social Exclusion: The Development of Consumer Oriented Initiatives in the European Union*, Dublin: The Foundation.

Evandrou, M. and Falkingham, J. (2005) 'A Secure 'Retirement for All? Older People and New Labour', in J. Hills and K. Stewart (eds) *A More Equal Society: New Labour, Poverty, Inequality and Exclusion*, Bristol: The Policy Press.

Evans, G. (2006) *Educational Failure and Working Class White Children in Britain*, London: Palgrave Macmillan.

Evans, K. and Fraser, P. (1996) 'Difference in the City: Locating Marginal Use of Public Space', in C. Samson and N. South (eds) *The Social Construction of Social Policy: Methodologies, Racism, Citizenship and the Environment*, Basingstoke: Macmillan.

Evans, T. and Harris, J. (2004) 'Street-level Bureaucracy and the (Exaggerated) Death of Discretion', *British Journal of Social Work*, vol 34, no 6, pp 871-96.

Fabriquant, M. and Burghardt, S. (1992) *The Welfare State Crisis and the Transformation of Social Service Work*, New York, NY: M.E. Sharpe.

Fagan, T. and Lee, P. (1997) '"New" Social Movements and Social Policy: A Case Study of the Disability Movement', in M. Lavallette and A. Pratt (eds) *Social Policy: A Conceptual and Theoretical Introduction*, London: Sage Publications.

Fahlberg, V. (1994) *A Child's Journey Through Placement*, London: British Association for Adoption and Fostering.

Fairclough, N. (1992) *Discourse and Social Change*, Cambridge: Polity Press.

Fairclough, N. (1995) *Critical Discourse Analysis: The Critical Study of Language*, London: Longman.

Faragher, E.B., Cass, M. and Cooper, C.L. (2005) 'The Relationship between Job Satisfaction and Health: A Meta-analysis', *Occupational and Environmental Medicine*, vol 62, pp 105-12.

Ferguson, I. and Lavalette, M. (2004) 'Beyond Power Discourse: Alienation and Social Work', *British Journal of Social Work*, vol 34, no 3, pp 297-312.

Fernandez, R.M., Castilla, E.J. and Moore, P. (2000) 'Social Capital at Work: Networks and Employment at a Phone Center', *American Journal of Sociology*, vol 105, no 5, pp 1288-356.

Field, J. (2003) *Social Capital*, London: Routledge.

Finch, J. and Groves, D. (eds) (1983) *A Labour of Love: Women, Work and Caring*, London: Routledge and Keegan Paul.

Fine, B. and Leopold, E. (2001) *The World of Consumption*, London: Routledge.

Fink, J. (2004) 'Care: Meanings, Identities and Morality', in J. Fink (ed) *Care: Personal Lives and Social Policy*, Bristol: The Policy Press.

Firat, F.A. (1994) 'Gender and Consumption: Transcending the Feminine', in A. Costa (ed) (1994) *Gender Issues and Consumer Behaviour*, London: Sage Publications.

Fischer, C. (1999) 'Uncommon Values, Diversity and Conflict in City Life', in N. Smelser and J. Alexander (eds) *Diversity and its Discontents: Cultural Conflict and Common Ground in Contemporary American Society*, Princeton, NJ: Princeton University Press.

Forsyth, B. and Jordan, B. (2002) 'The Victorian Ethical Foundations of Social Work in England – Continuity and Contradiction', *British Journal of Social Work*, vol 32, no 7, pp 847-62.

Foucault, M. (1977) *Discipline and Punish*, Harmondsworth: Penguin.

Foucault, M. (1984) *The History of Sexuality: Volume 1: An Introduction*, Harmondsworth: Penguin.

Foucault, M. (1994) *Power: Essential Works of Foucault 1954-84 edited by Faubion, J*, Harmondsworth: Penguin.

Franklin, B. (ed) (1995) *The Handbook of Children's Rights*, London: Routledge.

Franklin, B. (ed) (2002) *The New Handbook of Children's Rights*, London: Routledge.

French, M. (1985) *Beyond Power: On Women, Men and Morals*, New York, NY: Summit Books.

Friedan, B. (1981) *The Second Stage*, New York, NY: Summit Books.

Friedman, A. (1977) *Industry and Labour: Class Struggle at Work and Monopoly Capitalism*, London: Macmillan.

Friere, P. (1996 [1970]) *Pedagogy of the Oppressed*, Harmondsworth: Penguin.

Fromm, E. (2002) *The Sane Society*, London: Routledge.

Froud, J., Johal, S., Leaver, A. and Williams, K. (2005) 'Different Worlds of Motoring: Choice, Constraint and Risk in Household Consumption', *Sociological Review*, vol 53, no 1, pp 96-127.

Fulcher, J. and Scott, J. (1999) *Sociology*, Oxford: Oxford University Press.

Gabriel, Y. and Lang, T. (1995) *The Unmanageable Consumer: Contemporary Consumption and its Fragmentation*, London: Sage Publications.

Gallie, D. (2002) 'The Quality of Working Life in Welfare Strategy', in G. Esping-Anderson (ed) *Why We Need a New Welfare State*, Oxford: Oxford University Press.

Gallie, D. and Russel, H. (1998) 'Unemployment and Life Satisfaction', *Archives Européennes de Sociologie*, vol XXXIX, no 2, pp 3-35.

Gallie, D., White, M., Chang, Y. and Tomlinson, M. (eds) (1998) *Restructuring the Employment Relationship*, Oxford: Clarendon Press.

Gans, H.J. (1968) 'Urbanism and Suburbanism as Ways of Life', reprinted in R. Bocock, P. Hamilton, K. Thompson and A. Waton (eds) (1980) *An Introduction to Sociology*, London: Fontana.

Garret, P.M. (1999) 'Mapping Child Care Social Work in the Final Years of the 20th Century: A Critical Response to the Looking After Children System', *British Journal of Social Work*, vol 29, no 1, pp 27-47.

Garret, P.M. (2002) 'Social Work and the Just Society: Diversity, Difference and the Sequestration of Poverty', *Journal of Social Work*, vol 2, pp 187-210.

Garret, P.M. (2004) 'The Electronic Eye: Emerging Surveillant Practices in Social Work with Children and Familes', *European Journal of Social Work*, vol 7, no 1, pp 57-71.

Garvie, D. (2001) *Far from Home. The Housing of Asylum Seekers in Private Rented Accommodation*, London: Shelter.

General Social Care Council (2006) 'Put Social Care Centre Stage in Social Exclusion Drive' (www.gscc.org.uk/News+and+events/Media+releases/Put+social+care+centre+stage+in+social+exclusion+drive.htm, accessed 11 September 2006).

Giddens, A. (1978) *Durkheim*, London: Fontana Press.

Giddens, A. (1982) *Sociology: A Brief but Critical Introduction*, Basingstoke: Macmillan.

Giddens, A. (1994) *Beyond Left and Right: The Future of Radical Politics*, Cambridge: Polity Press.

Gilligan, C. (1982) *In a Different Voice*, Cambridge, MA: Harvard University Press.

Gilroy, P. (1987) *There Ain't No Black in the Union Jack*, London: Hutchinson.

Ginn, J., Street, D. and Arber, S. (eds) (2001) *Women, Work and Pensions: International Issues and Perspectives*, Buckingham: Open University Press.

Glasby, J. and Littlechild, R. (2002) *Social Work and Direct Payments*, Bristol: The Policy Press.

Glass, N. (1999) 'Sure Start: The Development of an Early Intervention Programme for Children in the UK', *Children and Society*, vol 13, no 4, pp 257-64.

Goldson, B. (2001) 'The Demonisation of Children: From the Symbolic to the Institutional', in P. Foley, J. Roche and S. Tucker (eds) *Children in Society*, Basingstoke: Palgrave Macmillan.

Gordon, D., Adelman, L., Ashworth, K., Bradshaw, J., Levitas, R., Middleton, S., Pantazis, C., Patsios, D., Payne, S., Townsend, P. and Williams, J. (2000) *Poverty and Social Exclusion in Britain*, York: Joseph Rowntree Foundation.

Gough, I. (1978) 'Marx's Theory of Productive and Unproductive Labour', in D. McQuarie (ed) *Marx: Sociology, Social Change, Capitalism*, London: Quartet Books.

Graham, H. (1983) 'Caring: A Labour of Love', in J. Finch and D. Groves (eds) *A Labour of Love: Women, Work and Caring*, London: Routledge and Keegan Paul.

Graham, H. (1993) *Hardship and Health in Women's Lives*, Hemel Hempstead: Harvester Wheatsheaf.

Gramsci, A. (2003) *Selections from the Prison Notebooks*, London: Lawrence and Wishart.

Grant, I., Yeandle, S. and Buckner, L. (2005) *Working Below Potential: Women and Part-time Work*, Working Paper Series No 40, Manchester: Equal Opportunities Commission.

Gregg, P., Harkness, S. and Machin, S. (1999) 'Poor Kids: Trends in Child Poverty in Britain, 1986-96', *Fiscal Studies*, vol 20, pp 163-87.

Griffiths Report (1988) *Community Care: Agenda for Action*. London: HMSO.

Guillemard A.-M. (1993) 'Older Workers and the Labour Market', in A. Walker, J. Alber and A.-M. Guillemard (eds) *Older People in Europe: Social and Economic Policies*, Brussels: Commission of the European Communities.

Habermas, J. (1987) *Theory of Communicative Action*, Cambridge: Polity Press.

Habermas, J. (1998) *The Inclusion of the Other: Studies in Political Theory*, Cambridge, MA: MIT Press.

Hall, S. (1988) 'The Toad in the Garden: Thatcherism among the Theorists', in C. Nelson and L. Grossberg (eds) *Marxism and the Interpretation of Culture*, Urbana, IL: University of Illinois Press.

Hall, S. (1992) 'The West and the Rest: Discourse and Power', in S. Hall and B. Gieben (eds) *Formations of Modernity*, London: Sage Publications.

Halmos, P. (1965) *The Faith of the Counsellors*, London: Constable.

Halmos, P. (1978) 'The Concept of a Social Problem', in *Introduction to Welfare: Iron Fist and Velvet Glove*, DE206 Units 1-4, Buckingham: Open University Press.

Hardiker, P. and Curnock, K. (1979) *Towards Practice Theory: Skills and Methods in Social Assessments*, London: Routledge and Kegan Paul.

Harris, J. (ed) (2001) *Tönnies: Community and Civil Society*, Cambridge: Cambridge University Press.

Harris, J. (2002) 'Caring for Citizenship', *British Journal of Social Work*, vol 32, no 3, pp 267–81.

Harris, J. (2003) *The Social Work Business*, London: Routledge.

Harris, J. (2006) 'Bottom of the Class', *The Guardian*, 11 April.

Haurant, S. (2006) 'Plastic Fantastic', *The Guardian*, 29 June.

Harvey, D. (1973) *Social Justice and the City*, London: Edward Arnold.

Heaseman, K. (1962) *Evangelicals in Action: An Appraisal of their Social Work*, Letchworth: Garden City Press.

Heyes, D. (2005) 'Home Care Staff Worst Hit as Stress and Injuries take a Toll', *Community Care On-line*, 31 March.

Hills, J. and Stewart, K. (eds) (2005) *A More Equal Society: New Labour, Poverty Inequality and Exclusion*, Bristol: The Policy Press.

HM Government (2004) *Every Child Matters: Change for Children*, London: The Stationery Office (http://www.everychildmatters.gov.uk/publications).

Hobsbawm, E. (1994) *The Age of Extremes: The Short 20th Century 1914–1991*, London: Michael Joseph.

Hoggett, P. (2000) 'Social Policy and the Emotions', in G. Lewis, S. Gewirtz and J. Clarke (eds) *Rethinking Social Policy*, London: Sage Publications.

hooks, b. (1989) *Talking Back: Thinking Feminist; Thinking Black*, Boston, MA: South End Press.

Houston, S. (2002) 'Reflections on Habitus, Field and Capital: Towards a Culturally Sensitive Practice', *Journal of Social Work*, vol 2, pp 7–27.

Howe, D. (1987) *An Introduction to Social Work Theory*, Aldershot: Ashgate.

Howe, D. (1995) *Attachment Theory for Social Workers*, Basingstoke: Macmillan.

Howe, D., Brandon, M., Hinings, D. and Schofield, G. (1999) *Attachment Theory, Child Maltreatment and Family Support: A Practice and Assessment Model*, Basingstoke: Palgrave Macmillan.

Hugman, B. (1977) *Act Natural: A New Sensibility for the Professional Helper*, London: Bedford Square Press.

Hunte, C. (2004) *Rampton Revisited, The Educational Experiences and Achievements of Black Boys in London Schools*, London: LDA Education Commission (www.lda.gov.uk/server.php?show=ConWebDoc.568).

Husband, C. (1995) 'The Morally Active Practitioner and the Ethics of Anti-racist Social Work', in R. Hugman and D. Smith (eds) *Ethical Issues in Social Work*, London: Routledge.

ILO (International Labour Office) The Director General (2006) *The End of Child Labour: Within Reach. Global Report under the Follow-up to the ILO Declaration on Fundamental Principles and Rights at Work*, Geneva: ILO.

Izumi, S. (2005) 'Use of Critical Consciousness in Anti-oppressive Social Work Practice: Disentangling Power Dynamics at Personal and Structural Levels', *British Journal of Social Work*, vol 35, no 4, pp 435–52.

Jack, G. (1997) 'An Ecological Approach to Social Work with Children and Families', *Child and Family Social Work*, vol 2, pp 109–20.

Jack, G. (2000) 'Ecological influences on parenting and child development', *British Journal of Social Work*, vol 30, pp 703-20.

Jacoby, R. (1999) *The End of Utopia: Politics and Culture in an Age of Apathy*, New York, NY: Basic Books.

Jahoda, M. (1982) *Employment and Unemployment: A Social-psychological Analysis*, Cambridge: Cambridge University Press.

Jenson, J. and Mahon, R. (1993) 'Representing Solidarity: Class, Gender and the Crisis in Social-Democratic Sweden', *New Left Review*, vol 201, pp 76-100.

Jones, C. (1997) 'British Social Work and the Classless Society: The Failure of a Profession', in H. Jones (ed) *Towards a Classless Society?*, London: Routledge.

Jones, C. (2001) 'Voices from the Front Line: State Social Work and New Labour', *British Journal of Social Work*, vol 31, no 4, pp 547-62.

Jones, C. and Novak, T. (1993) *Poverty, Welfare and the Disciplinary State*, London: Routledge.

Jones, C., Ferguson, I., Lavalette, M. and Penketh, L. (2004) *Social Work and Social Justice: A Manifesto for a New Engaged Practice*, Liverpool: University of Liverpool (www.liv.ac.uk/ssp/Social_Work_Manifesto.html).

Jones, H. (ed) (1997) *Towards a Classless Society?*, London: Routledge.

Jordan, B. (2001) 'Tough Love: Social Work, Social Exclusion and the Third Way', *British Journal of Social Work*, vol 43, no 4, pp 527-46.

Jordan, B. with Jordan, C. (2000) *Social Work and the Third Way: Tough Love as Social Policy*, London: Sage Publications.

Jordan, B. and Parton, N. (eds) (1983) *The Political Dimension of Social Work*, Oxford: Blackwell Publishing.

Jordan, Z.A. (ed) (1972) *Karl Marx*, London: Nelson University Paperbacks.

Joyce, P., Corrigan, P. and Hayes, M. (1988) *Striking Out: Trade Unionism in Social Work*, Basingstoke: Macmillan.

Khan, P. and Dominelli, L. (2000) 'The Impact of Globalization on Social Work in the UK', *European Journal of Social Work*, vol 3, no 2, pp 95-108.

Keegan, W. (2006) 'Sterling News? Ask the Germans', *The Observer*, 2 April.

Kirsch, J. (2003) 'Metro-sexual Man Embraces Feminism', Euro RSCG Worldwide News Release, 15 June (www.prnewswire.co.uk/cgi/news/release?id=103873).

Koch, M. (2001) 'In Search of a Class Theory of Marginality and Exclusion', *International Journal of Contemporary Sociology*, vol 38, no 2, pp 193-212.

Kofman, E. and Sales, R. (1998) 'Migrant Women and Exclusion in Europe', *European Journal of Women's Studies*, vol 5, no 3-4, pp 381-98.

Langan, M. (1998) 'Radical Social Work', in R. Adams, L. Dominelli and M. Payne (eds) *Social Work: Themes, Issues and Critical Debates*, London: Macmillan.

Laslett, P. and Wall, R. (1972) (eds) *Household and Family in the Past Time*, Cambridge: Cambridge University Press.

Latouche, S. (1993) *In the Wake of the Affluent Society: An Exploration of Post-development*, London: Zed Books.

Lauglo, J. (2000) 'Social Capital Trumping Class and Cultural Capital? Engagement with School among Immigrant Youth', in S. Baron, J. Field and T. Schuller (eds) *Social Capital: Critical Perspectives*, Oxford: Oxford University Press.

Leadbetter, C. (1997) *The Rise of the Social Entrepreneur*, London: Demos.

Lee, M. (1993) *Consumer Culture Reborn*, London: Routledge.

Lee, P. (1982) 'Contemporary and Perennial Problems', in R. Bailey and P. Lee (eds) *Theory and Practice in Social Work*, Oxford: Blackwell Publishing.

Le Grand, J. (1990) *Quasi-Markets and Social Policy: Studies in Decentralisation and Quasi Markets Number 1*, Bristol: School for Advanced Urban Studies, University of Bristol.

Lenagan, I. (2006) 'Will Rugby League ever be Successful in the South?', *The Guardian*, 8 February.

Lentell, H. (1998) 'Families of Meaning: Contemporary Discourses of the Family', in G. Lewis (ed) *Forming Nation, Framing Welfare*, London: Routledge.

Leonard, D. and Speakman, M. (1986) 'Women in the Family: Companions or Caretakers?', in V. Beechey and E. Whitelegg (eds) *Women in Britain Today*, Milton Keynes: Open University Press.

Letwin, O. (2006) 'Why we have Signed up to Labour's Anti-poverty Target', *The Guardian*, 11 April.

Lewis, G. (2000) *'Race', 'Gender', Social Welfare: Encounters in a Post Colonial Society*, Cambridge: Polity Press.

Lewis, J. (2000) 'Gender and Welfare Regimes', in G. Lewis, S. Gewirtz and J. Clarke (2000) *Rethinking Social Policy*, London: Sage Publications.

Lewis, J. and Åström, G. (1992) 'Equality, Difference, and State Welfare: Labour Market and Family Policies in Sweden', *Feminist Studies*, vol 18, no 1, pp 59-87.

Lewis, J. and Glennerster, H. (1996) *Implementing the New Community Care*, Buckingham: Open University Press.

Lister, R. (2004) *Poverty*, Cambridge: Polity Press.

Littlewood, B. (2004) 'Women and Work: New Patterns and Directions', in P. Littlewood, I. Glorieux and I. Jonsonn (eds) *The Future of Work in Europe*, Aldershot: Ashgate.

Lloyd, K. (1993) 'Depression and Anxiety amongst Afro-Caribbean General Practice Attenders in Britain', *International Journal of Geriatric Psychiatry*, vol 39, pp 1-9.

Lloyd, K. (1998) 'Ethnicity, Social Inequality and Mental Illness: In a Community Setting the Picture is Complex', *References*, vol 316, pp 7147-63.

Loney, M. (1983) *Community against Government: The British Community Development Project 1968-78*, London: Heinemann.

Lunt, P. and Livingstone, S. (1992) *Mass Consumption and Personal Identity*, Buckingham: Open University Press.

Lury, C. (1996) *Consuming Cultures*, Cambridge: Polity Press.

MacDonald, C. and Jones, A. (2000) 'Reconstructing and Reconceptualising Social Work in the Emerging Milieu', *Australian Social Work*, vol 53, no 3, pp 3-11.

Macintyre, S., McIver, S. and Sooman, A. (1993) 'Area, Class and Health: Should we be Focusing on Places or People?', *Journal of Social Policy*, 22, pp 213-34.

MacLeod, D. (1888) 'On Non-Church Going and Housing of the Poor in Glasgow', reprinted in J. Moore (ed) (1988) *Religion in Victorian Britain: Volume III: Sources*, Manchester: Manchester University Press.

MacLeod, E. and Saraga, E. (1988) 'Challenging the Orthodoxy: Towards a Feminist Theory and Practice', *Feminist Review*, 28, pp 16-55.

Madanipour, A., Cars, G. and Allen, J. (eds) (1998) *Social Exclusion in European Cities*, London: Jessica Kingsley.

Majendie, P. (2006) *Pink Pound Prospers in the UK* (www.thisistravel.co.uk/travel/news/-Pink-pound-prospers-in UK_article.html?in_article_id =46060&in_page_id=143, accessed 10 November 2006).

Maloney, W., Smith, G. and Stoker, G. (2000) 'Social Capital and Associational Life', in S. Baron, J. Field and T. Schuller (eds) *Social Capital: Critical Perspectives*, Oxford: Oxford University Press.

Mama, A. (1989) *The Hidden Struggle*, London: London Race and Housing Research Unit.

Marwick, A. (1970) *The Nature of History*, London: Macmillan.

Marx, K. (1844) 'Contribution to the Critique of Hegel's Philosophy of Right', in K. Thompson and J. Tunstall (eds) (1983) *Sociological Perspectives*, Harmondsworth: Penguin Books.

Marx, K. (1970) *The German Ideology*, London: Lawrence and Wishart.

Marx, K. (1990) *Capital Volume I: A Critique of Political Economy*, London: Penguin Classics.

Marx, K. (1993) *The Grundrisse: Foundations of the Critique of Political Economy*, translated with a foreword by Martin Nicolaus, London: Penguin Books, in association with New Left Review.

Marx, K. (2005) *The Eighteenth Brumaire of Louis Bonaparte*, New York, NY: Mondial.

Marx, K. and Engels, F. (1992) *The Communist Manifesto*, Oxford: Oxford University Press.

Mayo, M. (1975a) 'Community Development: A Radical Alternative?', in R. Bailey and M. Brake (eds) *Radical Social Work*, London: Edward Arnold.

Mayo, M. (1975b) 'The History and Early Development of CDP', in R. Lees and G. Smith (eds) *Action Research in Community Development*, London: Routledge and Kegan Paul.

McClenaghan, P. (2000) 'Social Capital: Exploring the Theoretical Foundations of Community Development Education', *British Educational Research Journal*, vol 26, no 5, pp 565-82.

McCracken, G. (1990) *Culture and Consumption*, Bloomington, IN: Indiana University Press.

McDowell, C. (1992) *Dressed to Kill: Sex, Power and Clothes*, London: Hutchinson.

McKnight, A. (2002) 'From Childhood Poverty to Labour Market Disadvantage', in J. Bryner, P. Elias, A. McKnight, H. Pan and G. Pierre (eds) *Young People's Changing Routes to Independence*, York: York Publishing Service.

McKnight, A. (2005) 'Employment: Tackling Poverty through "Work for those who Can"', in J. Hills and K. Stewart (eds) *A More Equal Society: New Labour, Poverty, Inequality and Exclusion*, Bristol: The Policy Press.

McKnight, A., Glennerster H. and Lupton R. (2005) 'Education, Education, Education ...: An Assessment of Labour's Success in Tackling Education Inequalities', in J. Hills and K. Stewart (eds) (2005) *A More Equal Society: New Labour, Poverty, Inequality and Exclusion*, Bristol: The Policy Press.

McRobbie, A. (1994) *Post-modernism and Popular Culture*, London: Routledge.

McRobbie, A. (1997) 'Bridging the Gap: Feminism, Fashion and Consumption', *Feminist Review*, no 55, Spring, pp 73–89.

McSherry, D. (2004) 'Which came First, the Chicken or the Egg: Examining the Relationship Between Child Neglect and Poverty', *British Journal of Social Work*, vol 34, pp 727-33.

Miles, S. (1998) *Consumerism as a Way of Life*, London: Sage Publications.

Miles, S. (2000) *Youth Lifestyles in a Changing World*, Buckingham: Open University Press.

Miles, S. (2001) *Social Theory in the Real World*, Buckingham: Open University Press.

Millet, K. (1970) *Sexual Politics*, New York, NY: Doubleday.

Millham, S., Bullock, R. and Cherrett, P. (1975) *After Grace, Teeth: A Comparative Study of the Residential Experiences of Boys in Approved Schools*, London: Human Context Books.

Millward, D. (2005) 'The Smart Way to Sell Cars to Gays', *The Daily Telegraph*, 10 December.

Milner, J. (1993) 'A Disappearing Act: The Differing Career Paths of Fathers and Mothers in Child Protection Investigations', *Critical Social Policy*, vol 38, pp 48-63.

Molyneux, M. (2002) 'Gender and the Silences of Social Capital: Lessons from Latin America', *Development and Change*, vol 33, no 2, pp 167-88.

Mooney, G. (ed) (2004) *Work: Personal Lives and Social Policy*, Bristol: The Policy Press.

Moore, R. (1974) *Pitmen, Preachers and Politics: The Effects of Methodism in a Durham Mining Community*, Cambridge: Cambridge University Press.

Moore, R. (1982) *The Social Impact of Oil: The Case of Peterhead*, London: Routledge and Kegan Paul.

Mort, F. (1996) *Cultures of Consumption. Masculinities and Social Space in Late Twentieth Century Britain*, London: Routledge.

Mouffe, V. (2000) 'For an Agonistic Model of Democracy', in N. Sullivan (ed) *Political Theory in Transition*, London: Routledge.

Muirhead, J.H. (1911) 'The City of Birmingham Aid Society', in J.H. Muirhead (ed) *Birmingham Institutions*, Birmingham: Cornish Brothers.

Muncie, J. (1999) *Youth and Crime: A Critical Introduction*, London: Sage Publications.

Murard, N. (2002) 'Guilty Victims: Social Exclusion in Contemporary France', in P. Chamberlayne, M. Rustin and T. Wengraf (eds) *Biography and Social Exclusion in Europe: Experiences and Life Journeys*, Bristol: The Policy Press.

Murray, C. (1984) *Losing Ground: American Social Policy, 1950-1980*, New York, NY: Basic Books.

Murray, C. (1990) *The Emerging British Underclass. Choice in Welfare Series, No 2*, London: Health and Welfare Unit, Institute of Economic Affairs.

Murray, C. (1994) *Underclass: The Crisis Deepens*, London: Health and Welfare Unit, Institute of Economic Affairs.

National Institute of Social Work (1982) *Social Workers. Their Role and Tasks* (The Barclay Report), London: Bedford Square Press.

Nazroo, J. (1997) *Ethnicity and Mental Health: Findings from National Community Survey*, London: Policy Studies Institute.

Nazroo, J. (1998) 'Rethinking the Relationship between Ethnicity and Mental Health: The British Fourth National Survey of Ethnic Minorities', *Social Psychiatry and Psychiatric Epidemiology*, vol 33, pp 145-8.

NHS Health Advisory Service (1995) *Together We Stand: The Commissioning, Role and Management of Child and Adolescent Mental Health Services*, London: HMSO.

Nisbet, R. (1967) *The Sociological Tradition*, London: Heinemann.

Nixon, P., Burford, G. and Edelbaum, A. (2005) *A Survey of International Practices, Policy and Research on Family Group Conferencing and Related Practices*, Family Rights Group (www.frg.org.uk/FGC/policy_and_research.asp, accessed 12 November, 2006).

Noble, C. (2004) 'Post-modern Thinking: Where is it Taking Social Work?', *Journal of Social Work*, vol 4, no 3, pp 289-304.

Oakley, A. (1985) *The Sociology of Housework* (revised edn), Oxford: Blackwell Publishing.

Oakley, A. (1987) 'Gender and Generation: The Life and Times of Adam and Eve', in P. Allatt, T. Keil, A. Bryman and B. Bytheway (eds) *Women and the Life Cycle*, London: Macmillan.

Oakley, A. (2005) *The Ann Oakley Reader: Gender, Women and Social Science*, Bristol: The Policy Press.

O'Brien, M. (2004) 'What is Social about Social Work?', *Social Work and Social Sciences Review*, vol 11, no 2, pp 36-53.

O'Hara, M. and Lee, A. (2006) 'Moving with the Times', *The Guardian*, 12 April.

Ojumu, A. (2004) 'The New Black', *The Observer*, 22 August.

O'Leary, N.C. and Sloane, P.J. (2005) 'The Return to a University Education in Great Britain', *National Institute Economic Review*, vol 193, no 1, pp 75-89.

Oliver, M. (1990) *The Politics of Disablement*, Basingstoke: Macmillan.

ONS (Office for National Statistics) (2003) *Victims of Crime* (www.statistics.gov.uk/cci/nugget.asp?id=467, accessed 11 November 2006).

ONS (2005) 'Education: Chinese Pupils have best GCSE results', (www.statistics.gov.uk/cci/nugget.asp?id=461, accessed 11 November 2006).

Owusu-Bempah, K. and Howitt, D. (2000) *Psychology Beyond Western Perspectives*, Leicester: British Psychological Society Books.

Palmer, G., Carr, J. and Kenway, P. (2005) 'Monitoring Poverty and Social Exclusion', York: Joseph Rowntree Foundation (the report can be accessed in PDF format at www.npi.org.uk/publications.htm).

Pantazis, C., Gordon, D. and Levitas, R. (2006) *Poverty and Social Exclusion in Britain: The Millennium Survey*, Bristol: The Policy Press.

Park, R. (1952) 'The City: Suggestions for the Investigation of Human Behaviour in the City', *American Journal of Sociology*, vol 20, pp 577-612.

Parker, H. (1974) *View From the Boys*, London: David and Charles.

Parsons, G. (ed) (1991) 'Victorian Roman Catholicism: Emancipation, Expansion and Achievement', in G. Parsons (ed) *Religion in Victorian Britain. Volume I. Traditions*, Manchester: Manchester University Press.

Parsons, T. (1951) *The Social System*, New York, NY: Free Press.

Parsons, T. (1954) *Essays in Sociological Theory*, New York, NY: Free Press.

Parsons, T. and Bales, R. (1955) *Family Socialization and Interaction Process*, New York, NY: Free Press.

Pearce, D. (1990) 'Welfare is not *for* Women', in L. Gordon (ed) *Women, the State, and Welfare*, London: University of Wisconsin Press.

Pearson, G. (1975) *The Deviant Imagination*, Basingstoke: Macmillan.

Pearson, G. (1983) *Hooligan: A History of Respectable Fears*, Basingstoke: Macmillan.

Penketh, L. and Ali, Y. (1997) 'Racism and Social Welfare', in M. Lavallette and A. Pratt (eds) *Social Policy: A Conceptual and Theoretical Introduction*, London: Sage Publications.

Perea, J. (ed) (1996) *Immigrants Out! The New Nativism and the Anti-immigrant Impulse in the United States*, New York, NY: New York University Press.

Perlman, H.H. (1972) 'Casework and "the Dimished Man"', in M. Fitzgerald, P. Halmos, J. Munice and D. Zeldin (eds) (1977) *Welfare in Action*, London: Routledge and Kegan Paul.

Phillipson, C., Bernard, M. and Strang, P. (1986) *Dependency and Interdependency in Old Age: Theoretical Perspectives and Policy Alternatives*, London: Croom Helm, in association with the British Society of Gerontology.

Phipps, J. and Hopwood Road, F. (2006) *Deeper in Debt: The Profile of CAB Debt Clients*, London: Social Policy Department, Citizens Advice Bureau.

Poulantzas, N. (1978) *Classes in Contemporary Capitalism*, London: Verso.

Power, A. and Willmott, H. (2005) 'Bringing up Families in Poor Neighbourhoods under New Labour', in J. Hills and K. Stewart (eds) *A More Equal Society: New Labour, Poverty, Inequality and Exclusion*, Bristol: The Policy Press.

Press Association (2005) 'Call for Separate Classes for Black Boys', *The Guardian*, 7 March.

Price, V. and Simpson, G. (2004) 'Values and Motivations: Why Become a Social Worker', Unpublished paper, University of Wolverhampton.

Pringle, K. (1995) *Men, Masculinities and Social Welfare*, London: UCL Press.

Putnam, R.D. (2000a) 'Bowling Alone: America's Declining Social Capital', *Journal of Democracy*, vol 6, pp 65-78.

Putnam, R.D. (2000b) *Bowling Alone: The Collapse and Revival of American Community*, New York, NY: Simon & Schuster.

Reamer, F.G. (1993) *The Philosophical Foundations of Social Work*, New York, NY: Columbia University Press.

Reay, D., David, M. and Ball, S. (2005) *Degrees of Choice: Social Class, Race and Gender in Higher Education*, Stoke-on-Trent: Trentham Books.

Rex, J. and Moore, R. (1967) *Race, Community and Conflict: A Study of Sparkbrook*, Oxford: Oxford University Press.

Rich, A. (1984) *The Fact of a Doorframe: Poems, Selected and New 1950–1984*, New York, NY: W.W. Norton.

Richards K. (2006) *Birmingham News*, 18 May.

Ridge, T. (2002) *Childhood Poverty and Social Exclusion*, Bristol: The Policy Press.

Ritzer, G. (1993) *The McDonaldization of Society*, Thousand Oaks, CA: Pine Forge Press.

Ritzer, G.J. and Goodman, D.J. (2004) *Sociological Theory* (6th edn), New York, NY: McGraw Hill.

Room, G. (1995) 'Poverty and Social Exclusion: The New European Agenda for Policy and Research', in G. Room (ed) (1995) *Beyond the Threshold: The Measurement and Analysis of Social Exclusion*, Bristol: The Policy Press.

Rowbotham, S. (1973) *Hidden from History: 300 Years of Women's Oppression and the Fight against it*, London: Pluto Press.

Rowbotham, S., Segal, L. and Wainwright, H. (1979) *Beyond the Fragments: Feminism and the Making of Socialism*, London: Merlin Press.

Rutter, M. (1972) *Maternal Deprivation Reassessed*, Harmondsworth: Penguin.

Rutter, M. and Giller, H. (1983) *Juvenile Delinquency: Trends and Perspectives*, New York, NY: Guilford Press.

Ryan, J. with Thomas, F. (1987) *The Politics of Mental Handicap*, London: Free Association Books.

Salisbury, H. and Upson, A. (2004) *Ethnicity, Victimisation, and Worry About Crime: Findings from the 2001/2 and 2002/3 British Crime Surveys*, London: The Home Office.

Sassi, F. (2005) 'Tackling Health Inequalities', in J. Hills and K. Stewart (eds) (2005) *A More Equal Society: New Labour, Poverty, Inequality and Exclusion*, Bristol: The Policy Press.

Saunders, P. (1981) *Social Theory and the Urban Question*, London: Hutchinson.

Saville, J. (1957) 'The Welfare State: An Historical Approach', in E. Butterworth and R. Holman (eds) *Social Welfare in Modern Britain*, London: Fontana.

Scharf, T., Phillipson, C., Smith, A.E. and Kingston, P. (2002) *Growing Older in Socially Deprived Areas*, London: Help the Aged.

Scourfield, J. (2003) *Gender and Child Protection*, Basingstoke: Palgrave Macmillan.

Scull, A.T. (1984) *Decarceration: Community Treatment and the Individual – A Radical View*, New York, NY: Rutgers University Press.

Seabrook, J. (1978) *What Went Wrong?*, London: Gollancz.

Searing, H. (2006) 'Social Exclusion: A Social Workers' View' (www.radical.org.uk/barefoot/socex.htm).

Seebohm, F. (Chair) (1968) *Report of the Committee on Local Authority and Allied Personal Services*, Cmnd 3703, London: HMSO.

Segal, L. (ed) (1983) *What is to be done about the Family?*, Harmondsworth: Penguin.

Senior, P. and Bhopal, R. (1994) 'Ethnicity as a Variable in Epidemiological Research', *British Medical Journal*, vol 309, p 327.

Sennett, R. (1977) *The Fall of Public Man*, London: Faber & Faber.

SEU (Social Exclusion Unit) (2004) *Creating Sustainable Communities*, London: Office of the Deputy Prime Minister.

Sewell, T. (2000) 'Beyond Institutional Racism: Tackling the Real Problems of Black Underachievement', in *Multicultural Teaching*, vol 18, no 2, pp 27-33.

Sewell, T. and Majors, R. (2001) 'Black Boys and Schooling: An Intervention Framework for Understanding the Dilemmas of Masculinity, Identity and Underachievement', in R. Majors (ed) *Educating our Black Children: New Directions and Approaches*, London: Routledge Falmer.

Shakespeare, T. (1993) 'Disabled People's Self-Organisation: A New Social Movement', *Disability, Handicap and Society*, vol 8, no 3, pp 249-64.

Shapiro, C. and Varian, H.R. (1999) *Information Rules. A Strategic Guide to the Network Economy*, Boston, MA: Harvard University Press.

Sheller, M. and Urry, J. (2000) 'The City and The Car', *International Journal of Urban and Regional Research*, vol 24, no 4, pp 737-58.

Silver, H. (1994) 'Social Exclusion and Social Solidarity: Three Paradigms', *International Labour Review*, vol 133, nos 5-6, pp 531-78.

Simmel, G. (1950) 'The Metropolis and Mental Life', in K. Wolff (ed) *The Sociology of Georg Simmel*, London: Collier Macmillan.

Simmel, G. (1971) *On Individuality and Social Forms*, Chicago, IL: University of Chicago Press.

Simpson, G. (2006) 'I'll Refer you on ... Case Management in the UK', Paper presented at Heinrich Pesch Haus Social Networks London Seminar, 25 September, London.

Sivananden, A. (2006) 'Attacks on Multi-cultural Britain Pave the Way for Enforced Assimilation', *The Guardian*, 13 September.

Smiles, S. (1997: unabridged reprint of 1866 edition) *Self Help: With Illustrations of Conduct and Perseverance*, London: Health and Welfare Unit, Institute of Economic Affairs.

Smith, D.J. (1997) 'Ethnic Origins, Crime and Criminal Justice', in M. Maguire, R. Morgan and R. Reiner (eds) *The Oxford Handbook of Criminology* (2nd edn), Oxford: Clarendon Press.

Social Exclusion Unit (2004a) *What is Social Exclusion?* (www.socialexclusionunit.gov.uk/page.asp?id=213, accessed 9 November 2006).

Social Exclusion Unit (2004b) *Facts and Figures* (www.socialexclusion.gov.uk/page.asp?id=118, accessed 12 November 2006).

Social Exclusion Unit (2004c) *Mental Health and Social Exclusion: Social Exclusion Unit Report Summary*, London: Office of the Deputy Prime Minister.

Specht, H. and Vickery, A. (1977) *Integrating Social Work Methods*, London: Allen and Unwin.

Spender, D. (1980) *Man Made Language*, London: Routledge and Kegan Paul.

Stacey, M. (1960) *Tradition and Change: A Study of Banbury*, Oxford: Oxford University Press.

Stedman-Jones, G. (1981) 'The Threat of Outcast London', in M. Fitzgerald, G. McClelland and J. Pawson (eds) *Crime and Society: Readings in History and Theory*, London: Routledge and Kegan Paul.

Stedman-Jones, G. (1984) *Outcast London: A Study in the Relationship Between Social Classes in Victorian Society*, Harmondsworth: Penguin.

Stedman Jones, S. (2001) *Durkheim Reconsidered*, Cambridge: Polity Press.

Steijn, B. (2004) 'ICT, Organisations and Labour in the Information Society', in P. Littlewood, I. Glorieux and I. Jonsonn (eds) *The Future of Work in Europe*, Aldershot: Ashgate, pp 31-48.

Stepney, P., Lynch, R. and Jordan, W.J.O. (1999) 'Poverty, Exclusion and New Labour', *Critical Social Policy*, vol 19, pp 109-27.

Stewart, K. (2005) 'Towards and Equal Start? Addressing Childhood Poverty and Deprivation', in J. Hills and K. Stewart (eds) *A More Equal Society: New Labour, Poverty, Inequality and Exclusion*, Bristol: The Policy Press.

Stewart, G. and Tutt, N. (1987) *Children in Custody*, Aldershot: Avebury.

Stewart, H. (2006) 'Hazard Lights on for World Economy', *The Guardian*, 17 August.

Sutton, C. (1994) *Social Work, Community Work and Psychology*, Leicester: British Psychological Society Books.

Surkemper, P. (2003) 'A Crisis in German Social Engagement?', Unpublished paper, FH Dortmund.

Swift, K. (1995) 'An Outrage to Common Decency: Historical Perspectives on Child Neglect', *Child Welfare*, vol 74, no 1, pp 71-91.

Tawney, R.H. (1961) *Religion and the Rise of Capitalism*, Harmondsworth: Penguin.

Taylor, A. (2006) 'Practitioners' Workloads are Rising Evaluation Finds', Community Care On-line, 2 May (www.communitycare.co.uk/Articles/2006/05/02/53724/ Practitioners'+workloads+are+rising%2c+evaluation+finds.html?key =WORKLOADS, accessed 18 May 2006).

Taylor, A., Kumar, S., Jerrom, C. and Dobson, A. (2004) 'Shelf stacker was paid 29p an hour', *Community Care* (www.communitycare.co.uk/Articles/2004/ 06/02/44970/Wednesday+2+June+2004.html, accessed 5 May 2000).

Taylor, C.J. (2006) 'Manchester United Divided: Identity Crisis', *When Saturday Comes*, April, pp 18-19.

Temko, N. (2006) 'Five Years on an Angry Town Finds a Fragile Peace', *The Observer*, 21 May.

Thatcher, M. (1987) in an interview for *Women's Own Magazine*, 31 October.

Thompson, N. (1997) *Anti-discriminatory Practice* (2nd edn), Basingstoke: Macmillan.

Todd, J. (2000) *Mary Wollstonecraft: A Revolutionary Life*, London: Weidenfeld and Nicholson.

Tomlinson, S. (2001) 'Ethnic Minorities and Education: New Disadvantages', in H. Goulbourne (ed) *Race and Ethnicity: Critical Concepts in Sociology*, London: Routledge.

Turning Point (2004) *Hidden Lives*, London: Turning Point.

Twigg, J. (2000) 'Social Policy and the Body', in G. Lewis, S. Gewirtz and J. Clarke (eds) *Rethinking Social Policy*, London: Sage Publications.

Ungerson, C. (1983) 'Why do Women Care?', in J. Finch and D. Groves (eds) *A Labour of Love: Women, Work and Caring*, London: Routledge and Kegan Paul, pp 31-51.

Ungerson, C. (1987) *Policy is Personal: Sex, Gender and Informal Care*, London: Tavistock.

Veblen, T. (1994) *The Theory of the Leisure Class*, Dover. Constable. (A version can be accessed online at http://xroads.virginia.edu/~hyper/VEBLEN/ veblenhp.html)

Vleminckx, K. and Smeeding, T.M. (eds) (2001) *Child Well-being, Child Poverty and Child Policy in Modern Nations: What Do We Know?* (revised edn), Bristol: The Policy Press.

Walby, S. (1990) *Theorizing Patriarchy*, Oxford: Basil Blackwell.

Walker, A. (2006) 'Re-examining the Political Economy of Aging', in J. Baars, D. Dannefer, C. Phillipson and A. Walker (eds) (2006) *Aging, Globalization and Inequality: The New Critical Gerontology*, Amityville, New York, NY: Baywood Publishing Company Inc.

Walker, A. and Walker, C. (1997) *Britain Divided: The Growth of Social Exclusion in the 1980s and 1990s*, London: Child Poverty Action Group.

Walker, A. and Maltby, T. (1997) *Ageing Europe*, Buckingham: Open University Press.

Walkerdine, V. and Lucey, H. (1989) *Democracy in the Kitchen*, London: Virago.

Wall, T.D. and Lischeron, J.H. (1977) *Worker Participation: A Critique of the Literature and Some Fresh Evidence*, Maidenhead: McGraw Hill.

Warde, A. (1994) 'Consumers, Consumption and Post-Fordism', in R. Burrow and B. Loader (eds) *Towards a Post-Fordist Welfare State*, London: Routledge.

Warr, P. (1987) *Work, Unemployment and Mental Health*, Oxford: Clarendon Press.

Warr, P. (ed) (2002) *Psychology at Work* (5th edn), London: Penguin.

Watts, R. (2000) 'Mary Carpenter: Educator of the Children of the "Perishing and Dangerous Classes"', in M. Hilton and P. Hirsch (eds) *Practical Visionaries: Women, Education and Social Progress 1790–1930*, Harlow: Longman, Pearson Education.

Webb, D. (1991) 'Puritans and Paradigms: A Speculation on the Form of New Moralities in Social Work', *Social Work and Social Sciences Review*, vol 2, no 2, pp 146-59.

Webb, S.A. (2003) 'Local Orders and Global Chaos in Social Work', *European Journal of Social Work*, vol 6 no 2.

Weber, M. (1992) *The Protestant Ethic and the Spirit of Capitalism*, London: Routledge.

Weich, S. and Lewis, G. (1998) 'Material Standard of Living, Social Class, and the Prevalence of the Common Mental Disorders in Great Britain', *Journal of Epidemiology and Community Health*, vol 52, pp 8-14.

Western Mail (2003) 'Metro-sexual and Proud', 21 June.

Whelan, R. (ed) (1998) *Octavia Hill and the Social Housing Debate: Essays and Letters by Octavia Hill*, London: Institute of Economic Affairs.

Whelan, R. (2001) *Helping the Poor: Friendly Visiting, Dole Charities and Dole Queues*, London: Civitas.

White, V. and Harris, J. (2001) *Developing Good Practice in Community Care: Partnership and Participation*, London: Jessica Kingsley.

White, V. and Harris, J. (2004) *Developing Good Practice in Children's Services*, London: Jessica Kingsley Press.

Whitehead, M. and Diderichsen, F. (2001) 'Social Capital and Health: Tiptoeing Through the Minefield of Evidence', vol 358, no 9277, pp 165-6.

Wieler, J. (2000) 'Social Pedagogical Family Help in Germany: New Wine in Old Vessels New Vessels for Old Wine?', in J. Canavan, P. Dolan and J. Pinkerton (eds) *Family Support: Direction from Diversity*, London: Jessica Kingsley.

Williams, F. (1997) 'Women and Community', in J. Bornat, J. Johnson, C. Pereira, D. Pilgrim and F. Williams (eds) *Community Care: A Reader* (2nd edn), Basingstoke: Macmillan.

Williams, F. (2001) 'In and Beyond New Labour: Towards a New Political Ethics of Care', *Critical Social Policy*, vol 21, no 4, pp 467-93.

Willis, P. (1978) *Learning to Labour*, Farnborough: Saxon House.

Wilson, E. (1977) *Women and the Welfare State*, London: Tavistock.

Winter, K. and Connolly, P. (2005) 'A Small-scale Study of the Relationship between Measures of Deprivation and Child-care Referrals', *British Journal of Social Work*, vol 35, no 6, pp 937-52.

Wirth, L. (1938) 'Urbanism as a Way of Life', *American Journal of Sociology*, vol 44, no 1, pp 1-24.

Wise, S. (1995) 'Feminist Ethics in Practice', in R. Hugman and D. Smith (eds) *Ethical Issues in Social Work*, London: Routledge.

Wright Mills, C. (2000) *The Sociological Imagination*, Oxford: Oxford University Press.

Yeates, N. (2001) *Globalization and Social Policy*, London. Sage Publications.

Young, M. and Willmott, P. (1957) *Family and Kinship in East London*, London: Routledge and Kegan Paul.

Zaretsky, E. (1976) *Capitalism, the Family and Personal Life*, London: Pluto Press.

Zukin, S. (1990) 'Socio-spatial Prototypes of a New Organisation of Consumption: The Role of Real Cultural Capital', *Sociology*, vol 24, no 1, pp 37-56.

Index

workplace-based stress 55–6
  and social work 59–60
Wright Mills, C. 1

Y

Yeates, N. 92
young offenders
  community care provisions 133–4
  historic attitudes 24–5
young people
  community care provisions 133–4
  and consumption patterns 105–6
Young, M. and Willmott, P. 68,118

Z

Zaretsky, E. 68
Zukin, S. 92–3